THIN ICE

THIN ICE

A Hockey Journey from Unknown to Elite—
and the Gift of a Lifetime

RYAN MINKOFF

LYONS
PRESS

Guilford, Connecticut

LYONS
PRESS

An imprint of The Rowman & Littlefield Publishing Group, Inc.
4501 Forbes Blvd., Ste. 200
Lanham, MD 20706
www.rowman.com

Distributed by NATIONAL BOOK NETWORK

British Library Cataloguing in Publication Information available

Library of Congress Cataloging-in-Publication Data available

ISBN 978-1-4930-3888-6 (cloth : alk. paper)
ISBN 978-1-4930-5842-6 (electronic)

♾™ The paper used in this publication meets the minimum requirements of American National Standard for Information Sciences—Permanence of Paper for Printed Library Materials, ANSI/ NISO Z39.48-1992.

CONTENTS

AUTHOR'S NOTE

SOME OF THE PEOPLE'S NAMES HAVE BEEN CHANGED TO PROTECT THE non-innocent from themselves. Where Finnish language appears, if grammatically or otherwise incorrect, I apologize. Enjoy my winding path through the hockey world.

Acknowledgments

THIS BOOK WOULD NOT HAVE BEEN POSSIBLE WITHOUT THE HELP AND support of my wonderful, loving family. I can't thank you enough for believing in me. I'd like to send a heartfelt thank you to a few special people.

Thank you to my parents, Jim and Kristie, who sacrificed so much to give me such a good start in life. They were so supportive in the ongoing development of this book these past few years as well. I hope this book makes you proud.

Thank you to my sister, Laura, for always being there as a friend and an outlet.

To my Lyons Press team, thank you for your hard work in putting this book together, and to Tom McCarthy, thank you for believing in my story from the very beginning.

An immense thank you to Vicki McCown, who inspired me to think deeper while editing my story and motivated me to become a better writer in the process.

To Patrick Krieger, I appreciate your added insights and perspectives while reviewing this book.

Thank you to Dan Treadway of the *Players' Tribune*, who believed in the value of my work when I sent in my first story on an August afternoon in 2015 and submitted my second in April 2016. You gave me a platform to get my writing career started, and I am forever thankful to you for reading my e-mails.

I want to thank my 83, LLC clients for being a part of my life. You have all impacted my growth both professionally and personally.

And finally, a huge thank you to my friends for being there for me and pushing me to pursue my dreams.

FOREWORD

I FIRST MET RYAN AS AN EIGHT-YEAR-OLD TEAMMATE ON THE "WEST" squad in the Minnesota SuperSeries, a spring hockey select tournament. I was a squirt in the Hopkins Youth Hockey Association and Ryan played with Buffalo Youth Hockey. After the tournament, Ryan's father formed the '93-born AAA Minnesota Lightning, a summer team made up of top players in the west metro area of the Twin Cities, and he recruited me to play for the inaugural team. David Backes, an NHL veteran, played for the '84 Minnesota Lightning. Little did I know that I would be on that same NHL stage one day. Growing up playing with Ryan on the Lightning for many years, I developed great chemistry with him on and off the ice.

When people ask me what I love most about the game of hockey, the answer is always the same: the relationships and the memories off the ice and in the locker room with my teammates and coaches. Hockey has provided me with the opportunity to get to know some distinguished people throughout my career. Ryan is one of those guys. If you want to hear about a unique hockey journey with crazy stories, witness his drive through challenging times, and understand the true passion that keeps us all in love with the game of hockey, then you will want to keep reading. Ryan's story has it all. I am so proud of him and grateful to call him my friend.

—#72 Travis Boyd
Washington Capitals (NHL)

PROLOGUE

I SCORED A GOAL ON MY LAST-EVER SHIFT LATE IN THE THIRD PERIOD in a 6–5 loss—a memorable ending to a tumultuous first pro season with Lapuan Virkiä in Finland. As I took off my skates in the chilly locker room after the game, I knew my playing career was over. I couldn't think about anything else as I sat in a state of sadness and reflection. The realization started to hit me that after nineteen years of playing the game I love, the time had come to move on.

After loading my equipment onto the team bus, I boarded and plopped down in an open seat midway down the aisle. My emotions ran wild—one minute feeling proud of my hockey career and all I had accomplished, the next engulfed by disappointment about how my final season had unfolded. One of my Finnish teammates caught me in a moping state as we rumbled away from the arena and handed me his flask filled with Salmiakki Koskenkorva, a licorice vodka popular in Finland. I took a swig and passed it back. It tasted like motor oil, and it went straight to my head.

Staring out the window into the snowy abyss, I thought I saw a short, chubby man in a red suit feeding his reindeer. I always wondered what Santa did to stay busy after Christmas. Then I reminisced about a significant moment the summer before my sophomore year of college. I sat in the locker room of the Minnesota Made Ice Center in Minneapolis, cooling down after a scrimmage with a bunch of guys who played in the NHL, AHL, ECHL, European leagues, and NCAA Division I programs. On paper, a club hockey player doesn't belong in the same stratosphere as these guys. But here I sat next to Marty Sertich, who was playing in Switzerland after spending time in the AHL and winning the Hobey Baker Award at Colorado College.

Marty struck up a conversation with me, and as we talked he said to me, "You know, you can be good enough to play in Europe if you keep working."

Not only did he help set my sights on pro hockey in Europe, but he treated me—a quiet guy who felt like I didn't fit in—with respect, like I was an equal among the guys in this star-studded locker room.

An hour and change later, the bus neared our little hometown of Lapua, Finland. Stepping off the bus, I overheard a teammate say, "*mikä matka*," which means, "What a journey." What a journey indeed.

As I walked back to my apartment, taking in the sights of all the quaint buildings and cottages glistening in the moonlight, I started to think back to how it all began.

PART ONE

MINNESOTA MADE

INTRODUCTION

I PLAYED HOCKEY WITH RYAN STARTING WITH THE MINNESOTA LIGHT-
ning at eight years old and continued all the way up through high school
at Benilde-St. Margaret's. Funny to look back on those days now. As you
get older, you come to realize how lucky you are to grow up with such
a good friend. Like all Minnesota kids, our days and nights were spent
together at the rink. More often than not, Ryan shut me down in one-
on-one drills. (He paid me to write that.) But in games when he didn't
want to give me the puck off the wall for a breakout pass, he would step
out in front of the net like he was ready to make the rush ... then decide
he didn't like what he saw and go right back around behind the net. Mind
you, he was not afraid to do this two or three times in a row. In all seri-
ousness, Ryan was a solid defenseman and very unselfish in his play, and
it feels just like yesterday Ryan was assisting on one of my goals.

Ryan was a tireless worker and a great teammate. I used to wear
number 66 with the Lightning, emulating my favorite player, Mario
Lemieux of the Pittsburgh Penguins. I laugh now, but at the time, that
number on my jersey resulted in plenty of opponents coming after me in
games. I didn't have any idea what I was doing; I just wanted to wear the
number. Ryan did know, and he was always mindful of it because when
they lined me up, I always knew Ryan had my back. His career was quite
the adventure, and he faced challenges other players did not. As his teammate, I can truly say much was unwarranted and out of Ryan's control.
But I can also tell you he never once complained. I am not surprised by all
that he has accomplished, and to this day, I know Ryan still has my back.

—Christian Horn
#10 Norfolk Admirals (ECHL)

CHAPTER ONE

First Stride

ALTHOUGH TOO YOUNG TO REMEMBER, I ATTENDED MY FIRST HOCKEY game at the ripe old age of six months. My parents had season tickets to the University of Minnesota Golden Gophers hockey team. Since they attended every game that season and each subsequent season, so did I.

Once I turned three, I even had my own seat at these games. The highlight that season was getting my picture taken with the Minnesota team mascot, Goldy Gopher. Goldy stood six feet tall, and from a distance, he seemed to be a fun and happy character. He always made me laugh with his antics—diving on the ice, slamming himself into the boards, and spinning his head around and around. To pull off those shenanigans and not get hurt, Goldy had to be quite the ice skater. But up close, he towered over me and scared me to death. I feared I might become his dinner. I thought he was a real-life mutant rodent. My dad had to convince me he wouldn't eat me, and I managed to will myself to have my picture taken with him.

During this season, my parents bought me my first pair of hockey skates. We went family skating each week, and I got my first taste of what it took to stay upright on slippery ice—certainly not as easy as the players made skating look. It took a lot of balance and skill, which I didn't yet have. I fell numerous times, and thankfully, because I was so small, it was a short drop. The rink supplied plastic chairs first-time skaters could hold onto and push around the ice. I learned the elementary skating technique of "push, touch, glide": pushing off the ice with my skate and extending my leg, then touching my other skate upon completion of the stride as I

5

brought it back to the ice, and then gliding with both skates before performing the same sequence with my other skate. Eventually, gripping my trusty chair, I could motor around the ice like a pro.

I turned four in the spring and had my first experience with organized sports playing on our local T-ball team. It was a big deal. We had baseball jerseys, pants, and socks, just like the big-league players wore. Everyone got a chance to hit the ball off a tee at home plate and then run to first base—or, for some of the players who didn't quite get it, into right field or toward their parents. After everyone on the team had a chance to hit, we'd take the field. No one kept track of outs. Being that these teams were made up of mostly four-year-olds and maybe a couple of five-year-olds, the chances of a ball making it into the outfield was zero. I was lucky to play somewhere behind second base. Of course, none of us could throw accurately, so even if we managed to miraculously pick up a ball hit to us, no one knew where the ball would end up. Most of the time in the field was spent daydreaming, watching dandelions bloom, and wondering what the postgame snack would be. If I were to sum up this experience in one word, it would be "boring." Baseball was not my first love.

The sport of hockey moves too fast to be boring. Players zip around at over twenty miles per hour and pucks are shot at speeds of near or over one hundred miles per hour. So naturally, I picked hockey to try as my next organized sport.

My hockey quest began that fall. After spending most weekends watching Golden Gopher hockey games, I decided the time had come to give hockey a try. With all of the family skating I'd done to prepare me, I felt ready for prime time. My parents signed me up with the Hanover Youth Hockey Association, a small community about an hour outside of the Twin Cities. Hanover had the best logo of any jersey I've ever worn—a feisty insect with a mean look on its face, showing its teeth and flapping its wings. And it had a long, sharp stinger. We were the Hanover Hornets. Because I was pretty small in size, there was only one jersey that wouldn't cover me from head to toe. It happened to be jersey number 1.

Before my first practice, we headed off to Play It Again Sports to get all of my equipment: helmet, breezers, pads—shoulder, elbow, and shin. I had grown since last year, so I needed a new pair of CCM skates. My very first real hockey stick was made of wood and came from Christian Brothers, a stick factory named after Roger and Billy Christian in Warroad, Minnesota, the place where the hockey gods lived (or so I thought). Christian Brothers made sticks for the general public as well as for NHL players like Ed Belfour and Jaromir Jagr.

At my first practice, I spent the hour skating around the arena like I had done with my parents. They also had chairs on the ice, so I felt right at home. My dad coached my mini mite (first-level) team, so that made the experience all the better. I also started to make friends with my fellow teammates. Our team was made up primarily of five- and six-year-olds. At age four, I was the youngest on the team, but that didn't seem to matter.

At the very next practice, once again on the ice with my dependable chair, I noticed that a number of the skaters on my team were not skating with chairs or help of any kind.

I turned to my dad and asked, "Do I have to skate with this chair?"

"Ryan," he replied, "if you don't want to use the chair, you can just let go of it."

With that, I pushed the chair aside and took off down the rink. I flew across the ice, skating faster than anyone else out there. I thought, *I just have to get a little bigger and a little older and I'll be playing for the University of Minnesota and then in the NHL. This is what I was meant to do.*

I learned a lot of the key skating skills during my first three years playing youth hockey, but not without some bumps along the way. Every player who wanted to play goalie was given an opportunity to do so. In the State of Hockey that is Minnesota, people often said that kids who wanted to play hockey but were not good skaters could be goalies. But my dad thought differently, believing it took a certain personality to be a successful goaltender. He felt that the best goaltenders were actually excellent skaters, which ran contrary to Minnesota youth coaching lore.

My dad was a goalie in college. I thought I could easily follow in his footsteps; however, he must have had other ideas for me. My chance to play between the pipes did come, but unbeknownst to me, my dad picked the game against the best team in our section, Mound-Westonka. For the first and last time in my life I put on the pads and played goalie. You could say this game seemed like a reenactment of Custer's Last Stand. I gave up something like twenty goals on twenty shots. I did make a glove save on a breakaway—or should I say the shot found its way into my glove. I would never have any desire to play in the net again. I ended up primarily playing defense for the rest of the season and decided I would focus on becoming the best defenseman on the ice.

While I was playing for Hanover, my family went through some very challenging times. My dad was diagnosed with cancer when I was just a first-grader. I remember getting ready to trick or treat wearing my awe-inspiring Batman costume when I heard the news. I had no idea what cancer was; I just knew I wanted to help my dad conquer it. When he started treatments, he lost all of his hair pretty quickly. Once he became bald, I decided I would buy him a baseball cap from different college teams to wear each week. Each Saturday afternoon, as we prepared to watch the college football games on TV, I would have a new hat for him to wear that matched a team playing in the featured game of the day. Mom and I put in our fair share of time at the cap stores that fall.

Collecting hats with my dad helped us form a close bond and especially helped us concentrate on the positive aspects of life, and baseball caps would always have a special meaning to me. Thankfully, he won his battle with cancer and has been healthy ever since.

The first summer hockey camp I attended was where the hockey gods lived, in Warroad, also known as Hockeytown, USA. Any other town that calls itself that—I'm talkin' to you, Detroit—is sadly mistaken. This small town on the Canadian border is a hallowed area for Minnesota kids and adults alike. There is so much hockey history there and in neighboring Roseau; as a number of players from these two communities played on the 1960 and 1980 US Olympic hockey gold medal teams, including Neal Broten and Roger, Billy, and Dave Christian. I loved Warroad. If I could have lived anywhere else growing up, it would have been here.

Warroad is the home of Marvin Windows (contributors to the Warroad Gardens Arena) and the Marvin family, who carry on a rich hockey tradition, most notably by US Olympian Gigi Marvin. My dad and I arrived in Warroad the night before camp, and when we checked in at the hotel, the clerk told us about a barbeque and fundraiser at the rink for all the campers, so we decided to go.

The spectacle that night is something we talk about to this day.

When we arrived, we found out we needed tickets; apparently this event was not really open to everyone. However, the nice lady checking tickets graciously told us to come in and then added two seats at the head table. We found ourselves sitting with Minnesota Gophers announcer and former University of Minnesota, Minnesota Fighting Saints, and Minnesota North Stars hockey coach Glen Sonmor; new Gophers head coach Don Lucia; Warroad High School head coach Cary Eades; and former NHL players Henry Boucha and Dave Christian. Grateful for the hospitality, we bought ten raffle tickets to support the fundraiser.

When it came time for the raffle, we were ready to listen for our numbers. There were all kinds of prizes: large televisions, barbeque grills, DVD players, patio furniture, golf clubs, and more. The emcee read the first number: "78!"

I looked down at my sheet of numbers and saw that I had the winning ticket. I looked at my dad. "Dad, I just won!"

"Way to go! Go pick out a prize."

As a six-year-old whose dad had just beaten cancer, I knew there was only one prize to pick: a Warroad hockey baseball cap. Everyone in the room started laughing, both shocked and amused at my choice. But I was thrilled to get this prize hat. When I got back to my seat, my father could only smile.

The emcee then read off the next selected number. I had this winning ticket also. What do you think I did? I picked out another hat. No one in the room could believe this. Incredibly, over the course of the raffle, I won five times. I picked all four hats that were available as prizes—or so I thought. When I won for the last time and there were no more hats, Wyatt Smith, a former player at Warroad High School and the University of Minnesota and then a player with the NHL's Phoenix Coyotes, took off his Coyotes baseball cap and offered it to me. When I gladly accepted, he autographed it too. What a heavenly moment.

Looking back, I can't believe my dad didn't help me pick out the prizes. He just let me walk up and pick out whatever I wanted. He could have gone home with a new TV or barbeque grill or golf clubs. Of course, this all happened in front of the camp staff, coaches, and other campers and their families. Seeing me pick out those hats instead of the high-priced prizes put smiles on a lot of people's faces that night.

The Gardens Arena, home of the Warroad Warriors High School hockey team, hosted the camp. After that camp, Warroad became my favorite high school team to root for, not only because they were always an exciting team, but they had my favorite high school logo—an Indian brave with two head feathers.

As my family continued to attend Gophers hockey games each weekend, I learned more and more about how to play the game. My dad would tell me to watch a certain player, and I would follow him the whole game, rifling off questions to my dad throughout. This was on Friday and Saturday nights; on Sundays we would go family skating in the afternoon at the Maple Grove Community Center.

At family skating my dad had my younger sister, Laura, and me skating around the faceoff circles, doing skating drills, playing catch with my hockey gloves, jumping over all the lines on the ice, and trying little tricks. That's where I learned how to skate with good form, refining my "Jordan Leopold–like" skating technique and developing a long, smooth skating stride. Leopold starred for the Golden Gophers from 1998 to 2002, and I followed his every move at each game I attended with my family. Because of all of the hockey I had watched since birth, I began picking up on the strategies and nuances of the game, learning to be in the right place at the right time and not having to scramble to get to where I should be on the ice. Some coaches thought I wasn't trying as hard as other players since they didn't see a short, fast, choppy stride performed by a desperate, scrambling player.

Family skating is one of my fondest memories growing up. I'd be the last one off the ice every time, often finishing up the session with a few hard laps around the rink. I also spent countless hours with my friend Reid Trousdale, who had a backyard rink that his dad flooded in the winter. We would play out there for hours until we couldn't see the puck anymore.

Unfortunately, a couple of years after I began playing for Hanover, the association merged with the Buffalo Youth Hockey Association. A larger town and a more prominent association, Buffalo did not welcome the Hanover players with open arms, creating a political mess for the Hanover kids who continued to play hockey with Buffalo. Hanover was a small, tight-knit community when it came to the youth hockey program. As a result, the Hanover parents were very protective of its program and the Hanover kids that played in it. Buffalo parents felt that Hanover families were generally more financially well off, and because all of the players from both associations eventually enrolled into the Buffalo hockey program—particularly in high school since both communities attended the same school— they believed that Hanover kids were taking spots that should belong only to Buffalo resident players. It became a classic case of wishing the kids could just play and have the parents stay home. To make matters worse, at an informal skate that year, I approached Henry Porter, head coach of the Buffalo Bison high school varsity team, and said, "Hi, Coach." To my surprise, he replied, "Ryan, you will never play for me." *A little young to be claiming my hockey fate*, I thought (I was seven). It was safe to say where he stood on the Hanover-Buffalo merger. Coach Porter also happened to be the coach in chief of Minnesota Hockey (the governing body of all things hockey in Minnesota), and he knew and worked with every hockey coach in the state. Needless to say, he had a lot of influence on my future path as I moved from level to level—and it wasn't positive.

Even given all the politics, the Buffalo squirt coaches were very competitive and requested that I move up early from the mite level to try out for the squirt "A" team.

The summer before these tryouts, I attended a weeklong hockey camp with my sister, Laura, in Grand Forks, North Dakota, the home of the University of North Dakota Fighting Sioux hockey team.

The university had just built a state-of-the-art arena, one that rivaled any NHL facility. The seats were upholstered in leather and the floors made of marble. Every bathroom had TVs so fans never had to miss a moment of the action. At the hockey camp, we were given a tour of the facilities and we were coached on the ice by Sioux head coach Dean Blais and many of his current players, including my favorite, T. J. Oshie, and Brock Nelson, who went to Warroad High School, along with Matt Smaby, Mike Commodore, Ryan Duncan, Jeff Panzer, Jonathan Toews,

Karl Goehring, Brandon Bochenski, Matt Frattin, Zach Parise—the list of great players I got to meet goes on and on, and North Dakota became—and still is—my favorite college hockey program. Before this camp, I wore number 3 because of Jordan Leopold, but afterwards I wore number 11 a lot because this was Parise's jersey number. I switched my allegiance from Minnesota to North Dakota and have been a devout Sioux fan ever since.

My dad bought Laura and me green helmets after the camp, the same ones worn by the Fighting Sioux players and one of my favorite mementos from my early hockey years. When it came time for the squirt tryout, I proudly wore my green Sioux helmet. Everyone else at the tryout wore their Buffalo black or white helmet. Little did I know that this would create a firestorm among the parents watching the tryouts. The evaluators had requested that everyone wear the same colors of everything so that no one would stand out. Although the parents of many of the players tried to subtly circumvent this rule by having their kids wear unmatched socks of different colors, I was pretty bold as the "kid with the green helmet." At the end of squirt tryouts, evaluators ranked me in the top ten (number eight), which should have automatically put me on the squirt "A" team. But not only was I from Hanover, I had also beaten out the kids of the two squirt "A" assistant coaches, who were from Buffalo, in the tryouts. So naturally, the coaches moved me down to the squirt "B1" team.

That season was memorable not for the caliber of my play, but for an event involving my dad. He had been named the head coach of the squirt "B1" team, primarily because the son of the Buffalo association's president was on this team and the president did not want Brian Hampton, another parent, to be the head coach. Brian was a Hanover parent who had the same disdain for Buffalo parents and players that Buffalo had for Hanover. My dad was one of the few people both associations seemed to be okay with, so my dad was assigned the head coaching role. Trying to extend an olive branch over the coaching situation, my dad spoke to Brian, who agreed to be the assistant coach. This would backfire big time because Brian was always very resentful toward Buffalo and my dad for not being named the head coach himself. He felt that he was superior to everyone when it came to coaching. Brian had expected that my dad would step aside after being named head coach so that Brian could run the team.

One night during the season, we were scheduled to play Wayzata, a strong team in the state. On the bench during warm-ups, Brian said to my dad, "I am going to take over and run this team. You don't need to be here."

Taken aback, my dad replied, "Brian, you have to respect the fact that I am the head coach. You weren't assigned to be the head coach, so we need to work together on things."

Brian responded, "Well, I'd rather get ejected from this game than stay on the bench coaching with you."

Brian, clearly trying to bully my dad to give in, was about to get his wish.

Just before the game, when the referees came by to introduce themselves, my dad said to them, "Hey guys, my assistant wants to get thrown out of the game today."

The officials laughed and said, "Are you kidding?"

"No, I'm not," my dad replied. "Ask him."

The refs turned to Brian and asked, "So you want to get tossed today?"

"Yeah."

"All right then, you're out of the game. Get off the bench."

Brian, who didn't think this would actually happen and was now fuming mad but holding it in, trudged off the bench and watched the rest of the game from the stands. We all looked at each other and couldn't believe what we were seeing. Watching him walk off the bench, we didn't know how to respond, so we started laughing.

Following the game, Brian came over to our home. My father answered the door and asked him what was up.

Brian said, "I don't like the way you're coaching and me not being in charge, so let's work this out like men. Step outside."

Listening from the kitchen, I thought, *Is this guy nuts?*

At first baffled, my dad realized Brian wanted to physically fight him for the head coaching job. Knowing my dad wasn't one to back down, I had to see for myself how this would play out. My dad refused to engage him, tried talking to him calmly for a couple of minutes, then finally just shut the door on him. Thankfully, Brian drove home—but that was the end of their friendship.

While this was a very contentious year, it proved to be just the opening act of what was yet to come during my squirt years. The craziness would move to another level in my second season playing squirts. As a naive eight-year-old, I wasn't really aware of all the politics involved going into tryouts. I just focused on doing my best on the ice and hoped to have a great season with my friends. The good news was that I did make the squirt "A" team this time. The bad news was our coaches were three young guys, recent graduates from local Division III schools, who were named the coaches by the high school coach, Henry Porter. I started the season getting a fair amount of playing time on defense, and then suddenly, for no apparent reason, I found myself sitting on the bench more and more as the season progressed. I couldn't understand what had changed. I continually got yelled at for mistakes on the ice, even when I wasn't on the ice at the time. I was the team's whipping boy.

That summer, my family and I ran into two of the coaches at the Minnesota State Fair, and they came clean. It seems that during a game about a month into the season, two parents—the president of the association and his best friend—bolted into the locker room to confront the coaches between periods. Unhappy that I, a Hanover kid, was getting equal ice time as their kids, told the coaches to play me much less for the remainder of the year. The coaches said those two parents directed them how to coach throughout the season with the goal of mentally torturing me and doing whatever was necessary to get me to quit. Adults bullying an eight-year-old to get him to quit sounded like the plot of a bad novel, and at first I couldn't believe they would actually do this.

After my second squirt season with Buffalo, I tried out for a Minnesota All-Star team called the Minnesota Pride. If I made the team, I would play in a tournament in Lake Placid, New York, home of the 1980 Olympic Winter Games and the unforgettable Miracle on Ice. I had tried out for the Pride the previous spring but didn't make the team. Although I took it hard, if I'm being honest, my skills didn't compare with those of the other players on the ice. I kept the maroon Pride tryout jersey in my hockey bag for the rest of my playing career to serve as a motivating reminder. Whenever I put on my gear for a game or practice, I would see that jersey and it would inspire me to always work hard.

My goal all season long was to improve enough to make this team. At this tryout, I played my best hockey, clicking on all cylinders. I made the team, which helped elevate my confidence, especially given the winter season I had just gone through.

This tournament could not have been more uplifting. Skating in the same arena where the US hockey team defeated the Soviet Union in dramatic fashion in the famous Miracle on Ice, we won the championship. The CAN/AM tournament had teams from both Canada and the United States. On an off day, I rocketed down the luge course the Olympians used in the 1980 Winter Games. To this day, that remains the best tournament I have ever participated in, and I am thankful to Bernie McBain, who created this opportunity and made lifelong memories for many hockey kids.

One of my Pride teammates was Jeff Spellmire. Jeff had an infectious, carefree attitude and a great sense of humor, which made him very enjoyable to be around. He was always trying to do goofy but harmless things, such as hiding teammates' pants after practice or squirting water at them during water breaks. He played in the Bloomington Jefferson Youth Hockey Association, a highly respected hockey program in Minnesota. Jeff left that association as a squirt to play with the Wisconsin Fire, a Tier I hockey organization located in Somerset, Wisconsin, that traveled and played throughout the Midwest. This program was much more comprehensive than what local youth hockey associations provided, practicing more often and longer every week, playing twice as many games during the season, and competing against some of the best teams in Michigan, Illinois, Missouri, and even Florida.

However, the Wisconsin Fire had some internal issues, such as parents and coaches not getting along—similar to the behavior I'd observed with Hanover and Buffalo. A couple of the parents (including Jeff's dad) decided they would start a new Tier I team—Team Midwest, based in River Falls, Wisconsin. Because I had gotten to know Jeff and his family, I had the opportunity to try out and play my first year of peewee hockey with Team Midwest, where Jeff was also playing. What a great alternative to playing in Buffalo—and on a team that wanted me.

Before I joined Team Midwest, I had one more year of squirt hockey to play, and I again made the squirt "A" team. This season I was coached by Jim Trousdale (my friend Reid's father) and my dad—the last season he would ever coach me. There were no parent or coach issues all season and everyone got along. All of the problem parents had moved on to the peewee level, and for some reason Henry Porter didn't have any interest in this squirt team. We won the elusive District 5 Championship—just like in the movie *The Mighty Ducks*—a title Buffalo teams had tried for years to win. It goes to show that when a team has synergy, supportive coaches and parents, and a positive environment, kids can accomplish greatness.

Thankfully, after that season my time at Buffalo came to an end. I loved all the kids on my teams and many of those in the association with whom I interacted. We all got along, both on and off the ice and at school. Some of us are still friends today. Notably, I spent many hours hanging out with Ben Aslesen from Buffalo, who was diagnosed with and overcame non-Hodgkin's lymphoma shortly after my squirt years. He was such a great friend to be around and very mentally tough. With Hanover natives Hunter Volbrecht and Nick Solorz, I had tons of snow-ball fights and memories of skating around on the Hanover outdoor rink in the frigid winters.

After the winter hockey season ended, one of our family's annual spring events was attending the WCHA Final Five hockey tournament, the Western Division I college league playoff that led up to the NCAA tournament. Hosted each year by the city of St. Paul, this event featured the top five teams in the league. The University of Minnesota, Wisconsin, North Dakota, and Denver were almost always there, it seemed.

We had season tickets to this tournament, and our seats were right on the glass near the penalty box. One of the refs was Hunter's dad, Bill Volbrecht, so countless pucks were tossed over the glass to me or my sister, which made the tournament more special. We grew a nice little collection of game pucks. I miss those days. That tournament's historic rivalries and energetic fans were unmatched. It no longer exists in its original format since the advent of the Big Ten Hockey Conference.

We also had tickets every year to the iconic Minnesota state high school hockey tournament. Our seats were in the first row, directly behind the player's bench. Whenever the coaches were interviewed on TV, my family could be spotted sitting in the background. The bad news about being directly behind the bench was the players and coaches were standing up all the time, so we had to watch the game on the center ice scoreboard half of the time.

Heading into the summer before my first peewee season, I attended the Back2Back Hockey Camp—named after the University of Minnesota's national championships in 2002 and 2003 and put on by players on those two teams: Joey Martin, Paul Martin, Jon Waibel, Grant Potulny, Troy Riddle, Matt Koalska, and others. I felt very lucky to have grown up only a mile away from Joey Martin. He would come over to my house while he was in college and offer me a lot of encouragement and advice. He also taught me how to shoot the puck like a champ. Joey was a great role model, and I appreciated his willingness to spend time coaching me and being so supportive.

A new adventure was about to unfold for me. Having left the Buffalo hockey program, I started down an unconventional hockey path, playing in a league outside the sanctioned Minnesota Hockey organization called Tier I hockey.

Tier I hockey is governed by USA Hockey and was not allowed to operate in the state of Minnesota per Minnesota Hockey, as they did not want another hockey organization to compete against their Minnesota state high school league. The one exception at the time was the famous Shattuck-St. Mary's, which helped develop the likes of Sidney Crosby, Zach Parise, and many other future stars. Minnesota is the only state in the United States with a powerful governing body, which operates as an affiliate of USA Hockey. The rest of the country is directed under USA Hockey. Minnesotans have a superiority complex when it comes to hockey and their development structure. It may be somewhat justified since Minnesota does produce the highest number of pro hockey players in the country and has the most current NHL players out of all of the states (thirty-two NHLers versus twenty from second-place Michigan as of the beginning of the 2019–2020 season).

I was off to Team Midwest, where I started playing at the peewee level. The team practiced and played home games in River Falls, Wisconsin, more than a ninety minutes' drive from my house—each way. For away games we traveled all over the Midwest, which made me feel kind of important. We were coached by Craig Norwich, an Edina, Minnesota, native who had played in the NHL and was a standout at the University of Wisconsin. He had textbook "hockey hair"—luscious, long blond locks—and a laid-back demeanor. He sometimes coached games wearing slippers on the bench. He knew the game and he knew how to coach, and that is what mattered most. Not only did I learn a great deal about the game from him, I developed as a player by facing great competition all season long in the Tier I Mid-America Hockey Association. I got faster and improved my vision, playmaking ability, and decision making. We played teams such as the Chicago Mission, Chicago Chill, St. Louis Jr. Blues, Florida Jr. Panthers, Madison Capitols, Team Wisconsin, and Wisconsin Fire. The year included plenty of eight-hour drives to Chicago, weekend flights, and a new insight into the game. Playing in that league elevated me into a confident young player and propelled me past my youth hockey contemporaries in skills and experience.

Like me, a number of my teammates were outliers from various Minnesota youth associations, so the parents and players all had similar backgrounds and could relate to each other. We developed great chemistry as a group. We really played like a team; everyone helped and pulled for each other on the ice and in the locker room. We carried an "us against the world" mentality into every game.

One player, Mack Mattke, was built like a truck and had a big-time shot and could run guys over. He came all the way from Cedar Rapids, Iowa, prompting everyone to call him "Cornfed" since he was the size of an Iowa corn field.

One of the founders of Team Midwest and an occasional coach we had, Stu Ronsberg, instilled in us the hard work and toughness needed to become a good player. In one game, Cornfed took a slapshot to the back of his leg and went down in pain. He laid on the ice like he was dead, not moving. Stu saw this and yelled, "Get up! Get up!"

Hearing Stu's voice echoing through the arena, Cornfed began to move.

Stu kept yelling, "Get up, Cornfed! Get to the bench!"

Cornfed, realizing he wasn't in fact dead—though in pain with a definite bruise on his leg—began to crawl and eventually made his way to his skates and onto the bench. Our whole bench stared at Cornfed as he came off the ice, just waiting to see what Stu would say to him next.

"Cornfed, you aren't dead. You're tough, way to get off." And Stu tapped him on the helmet. Though he instilled fear in many of us at practice, Stu had a way of always being positive during games and he always got the best out of us.

Stu would have us doing a simple neutral zone regroup drill—for 75 percent of a practice sometimes—until we were nearly perfect. He would put us through endless skating drills until we wanted to puke. He was so intense. There were times I hated his guts because he ran us so hard, but I knew deep down he was making me a better player.

I played defense all season against a much higher level of competition than just about everyone in the state of Minnesota. Because we were one of the weaker teams in the league, however, we got crushed a few times during this season. Our worst loss came against the best team in the league, the Chicago Chill, who held nothing back and beat us, 18–1. I remember this game for another reason: The coaches moved me from defense to center after the first period of the game. I had never played this position before, even in Buffalo or Hanover. I'd say this wasn't a very smart move on the coaches' part, considering we were facing the strongest team in the league. Then again, we were getting smoked, so it didn't matter what position I played. My weak play must have showed, though, as this was my first and last appearance at center that season.

Everyone in my family made sacrifices that year to get me to my practices and games. My dad drove me everywhere under the sun, a tremendous commitment of time and expense, while my mom drove my sister all over the state for hockey, ran her in-home daycare and preschool, and took care of the house and other commitments. Neither my mom nor my sister will tell you they enjoyed that year very much because dad and I were rarely around. The good news for our family dynamics was that the team folded after one season.

Playing with Team Midwest put a real wrench in my friendships with players from Hanover and Buffalo. I graduated from Hanover Elementary School after fifth grade and moved on to Buffalo Middle School for sixth. I never felt I fit in very well there. It was a much bigger school, and I didn't feel challenged by the coursework. Unfortunately, due to enrollment numbers, I wasn't able to join the Buffalo Community Middle School Honors Program, even though I was academically eligible. I had tested into Quest, which was the name of the honors program, but Quest took only a limited number of students, most of whom resided in Buffalo. During the school year, I wanted to leave for another school that would be more challenging and engaging, like the schools many of my teammates from Team Midwest attended.

That spring, I toured two private schools: Providence Academy and Benilde-St. Margaret's. Providence Academy was a newly opened Catholic school with fewer than one hundred students. The school required uniforms and seemed too preppy and strict for my liking. Benilde-St. Margaret's, also Catholic, didn't require uniforms, had better athletic programs, and seemed like a friendlier environment. My dad knew Chris Bonvino, who ran the custom jersey manufacturer Gemini Athletic, and worked with him on jersey orders for teams I had played on. Chris happened to be the assistant hockey coach under Larry Hendrickson with the BSM varsity team when I was considering the school. Because I sent in my application to BSM Junior High after the application deadline date, I wasn't able to take the entrance exams. However, Chris put in a strong reference to the school on my behalf, which, along with my solid Buffalo school transcript, secured my acceptance to the school a couple of weeks later. We actually knew someone willing to help me, so politics worked in my favor in this instance.

While BSM only had a high school hockey program, I very much looked forward to being able to play for Chris one day. Unfortunately for me, Chris Bonvino and Larry Hendrickson both left the BSM coaching staff a year later.

After my sixth-grade year at Buffalo Middle School, I said goodbye and moved to Benilde-St. Margaret's in St. Louis Park, Minnesota, about forty minutes away. Since my house was outside of the bus pickup zone, I had to be driven to school. Luckily, my parents found another BSM family that could help get me to school every day. Patty Gilmore, who worked as the head of the college and career center at BSM, lived only a couple of miles away from my home. I rode each day with her and her son Jon, who attended BSM High School.

The Gilmores, a welcoming and caring family, helped me make a smooth transition into the new school. I felt scared to be leaving the school and friends I'd known all my life but was excited for the challenge ahead. Benilde-St. Margaret's, one of the best college preparatory schools in Minnesota, would provide me a top-notch education. In my family, education was the number one priority, a value instilled in my sister and me by my parents.

When Team Midwest folded after my one season, I lost the opportunity for a great potential path to get to the Division I level. We had to figure out where I would play hockey the next season. Under Minnesota rules, I had to return to my home association—Buffalo. If the coaches and parents had hated me when I was there before, I could imagine how I would be treated on my return, so this was not an option. My dad worked out an agreement where Buffalo signed a waiver and let me go to an association outside the district willing to take me. We found an association on the brink of folding because it did not have enough players to field a team. The Tri-City Hockey Association warmly welcomed me.

Columbia Arena, where the movie *The Mighty Ducks 3* was filmed, would be my next new but short-lived hockey home. The towns of Tri-City—Fridley, Columbia Heights, and Brooklyn Center—bordered North Minneapolis. Of the four tournaments we played in that season, we won three, making it one of the most successful years a Tri-City team ever had.

I will never forget an exhibition game we played near the end of the season against the Wisconsin Fire 1995 team. Every kid on that team was at least two years younger than we were, so it should have been no contest, as that big an age difference is significant. But not this game. We lost at home, 4–1. Following the game, our irate head coach, Bud Williams, said, "You should all walk out of this arena with paper bags over your heads!" What a great line. He felt embarrassed about the loss and he made sure we did too.

To conclude our season, we played in the district tournament, facing off against Osseo. Right from the first shift, I knew I had a target on my back, as I got absolutely blown up at center ice even though I didn't have the puck—a cheap hit, making it clear they were deliberately coming after me. A couple of shifts later, I scored. That pretty much ended my night in the first period, because on the ensuing shift I was knocked out of the game by a hit in my own defensive zone, again nowhere near the puck. Osseo's head coach admitted after the game that he had directed his players to do what they had to do to get me out of the game. The coach felt that I was a ringer of sorts for the Tri-City program and that I shouldn't be playing with them.

Following that season, the Tri-City program folded and Columbia Arena was slated to be demolished to make room for a new housing development. So once again, I had to find a new association or I would be forced to go back to play for Buffalo.

But before finding my new home for the next season, I spent the heart of summer at a camp called International Hockey Schools in Detroit Lakes, Minnesota. Many of the kids in the camp stayed in a little dorm, but I stayed with my dad and sister in a nice hotel. At this camp I learned little skating tricks and more about how to play the game. Vladislav Tretiak, the legendary former Soviet Union goaltender, ran the goalie portion of the camp. My dad made sure to take a picture of my sister and me with him and had him sign it. I had a poster up in my room of him too. Meeting him—the first Russian I had met in my life—was really cool given my family history: Our last name, being of Russian origin, was spelled Minkov when my great grandparents immigrated to America, but when they arrived at Ellis Island, an immigration agent misspelled it. I always had an affinity toward Russian hockey and its history. Perhaps it was my way to get back to my ancestral roots. The moment was probably even sweeter for my dad because Tretiak had been his favorite goalie when he was growing up.

After this camp, my family worked their magic to find me a new association. This time, however, Buffalo would not agree to give me a waiver. I had two Bantam years left of youth hockey before playing in high school, and it looked like I'd be stuck in Buffalo. My parents got creative and found an interpretive loophole in the MN Hockey rules that would allow me to play in the Armstrong-Cooper Bantam program. The great lengths parents will go for their kids—I promised I would not disclose what they had to do in this book, but I am extremely appreciative.

This was a challenging two years for my parents as once again, my dad had to run me all around while my mom did the same for my sister. Laura continued to play in Buffalo. Once I left Buffalo, the association's negative focus shifted to my sister only slightly. The situation wasn't ideal for her, but unfortunately, she did not have the options I did to leave for another association that would accept her, nor would Buffalo give her a waiver.

On Wednesday mornings, I started my day at 6:00 a.m. on the ice at the Plymouth Ice Center with Karn Skating Dynamics. Former figure skater Jody Karn and her husband, Barry, an NHL skating coach for multiple teams, held a half-hour session to work with kids improving their skating skills. I started at this with this program when I was six years old and stayed for about eight years. It kept my skating ability really sharp, and I learned a lot of skating tips from them that I used throughout my hockey career and still use today.

I made the bantam "A" team both years I played for Armstrong-Cooper, coached by Duke Johnson and Mike Schone, two hard-nosed, no-nonsense guys who pushed me to keep getting better each day. I put up some big numbers those years, along with teammates Patrick Steinhauser, Christian Horn, and Dan Pemberton, all of whom also attended Benilde-St. Margaret's and eventually played in the BSM hockey program. With that, my youth hockey career came to a close. I had spent ten years bouncing among five different teams—from Hanover to Buffalo to Team Midwest to Tri-City to Armstrong-Cooper. I was a walking suitcase in youth hockey—seemingly a "rent-a-player."

As much as I bounced around during my youth winter hockey seasons, I was on the same summer hockey team—the Minnesota Lightning—from squirts through bantams. The Lightning, started by Jim Trousdale and my dad when I was eight years old—was one of the top AAA summer all-star traveling teams in the state. The team was made up of very strong players who lived primarily in the western suburbs of Minneapolis. Many of my fellow players on this team went on to play in college and a few played in the NHL, most notably Jonny Brodzinski and Travis Boyd.

Bud Williams was the head coach, the same coach I had in Tri-City. I have never met anyone like this man before. His famous saying was, "If you ain't cheatin', you ain't tryin'." He applied this saying to tricks he taught us on the ice to slow down an opposing player or knock somebody to the ice in front of the net. Coach Williams was a character; he always had his chewing tobacco and coffee in hand. He also had a son on the team, Brian, who I played a lot of defense with. Brian was known for his hip check that sent players flying over his back. Sometimes he got called for tripping because he dropped his body down so low that players flipped right over him. It was sweet seeing him throw that check. I enjoyed being paired with Brian.

Coach Williams taught me a lot about the game and toughened me up mentally. He let me know when I made a mistake on the ice by yelling when I got to the bench. As a pretty quiet kid, I did not like being on the receiving end of those tirades. I remember playing many games where my main goal was to avoid Bud Williams's wrath. Ironically, each time I did this, I ended up getting it. There were times I cried on the way home from games.

I had to grow a thick skin at a young age to tune out coach Williams when I screwed up on the ice. He would call me out and scream at me in front of the team, both on the bench and in the locker room. If I played a great game but had one subpar shift, he would relentlessly go off on me about that one shift. He definitely made playing hockey miserable at times, and I really had to push through all the negativity to stay motivated to play on the Lightning. During one game we played in Brandon, Manitoba, I got hurt and did not play the third period. I sat at the end of the bench to stay out of Bud Williams's way.

Our team had the lead going into the third period, but when we gave up the tying goal, Bud Williams came over to me twenty seconds later and got right in my face.

"See that Mink?" he screamed. "Your screwup is gonna cost us!"

"But Dad," protested Brian, "Ryan's not even playing. He's hurt."

"Doesn't matter. He shouldn't be some wuss just sittin' on the bench!"

We ended up losing that game—according to coach Williams—because of my poor play in the third period. Every coach seemingly has a whipping boy, and I took the brunt of it for most of my time playing with the Lightning.

The two assistant coaches on the team were Sam Swanson and Zack Little. Coach Swanson, a relatively quiet guy, primarily worked with defensemen, of which I was one along with his son Nick. Sam Swanson made sure he shielded his son from the wrath of the other two coaches by occasionally pairing me with Nick in games. When I skated with Nick, coach Swanson knew his son had carte blanche on the ice because if anything went wrong on that shift, I'd be the one to catch hell for it, no matter whether I was anywhere near the play.

Our harshest coach was Zack Little—an extreme perfectionist with an explosive temper. His famous frustrated yell was, "Holy Hannah, hit the net!" whenever a shot we took was not on goal. Coach Little hardly ever provided any constructive coaching tips. He seemed to enjoy yelling at players, making us feel inept and pointing out every mistake (no matter how trivial) we made during a game. No one on the team lived up to his standards, especially his son Trey, who was a forward. I caught my share of crap from Coach Little, but at least I wasn't singled out by him. I'm not sure I ever saw him smile on the bench. We had a very "glass half empty" group of coaches—unless those glasses contained beer.

In every tournament medal round we inevitably seemed to play the Minnesota Predators, arguably the top AAA team in the state at the time. We always played very competitive games against them, but then found some incredible way to lose in the third period. As we sat in the locker room before one of our epic battles with the Predators, Travis Boyd was wearing a baseball cap slightly tilted to one side, feeling hip and cool. Coach Little spotted it and screamed, "Travis, fix your hat or take it off! Are you serious? Don't you know how to wear a hat?"

After Zack Little left the locker room and our team laughed about his little blowup, Travis turned his cap and put it on backward. (This may be why Travis made it to the NHL—he had great skills, self-confidence, and just plain moxie to the point where no one ever intimidated him.) When Coach Little returned and saw how Travis was now wearing his cap, you could almost see the smoke coming out of his ears. Travis was saved by Bud Williams, who came in right behind Zack Little and addressed the team with his pregame speech. Coach Williams liked to end his talks with, "Okay, men, saddle up and put on your hats. It's time to ride." His parting words always put a smile on our faces as we headed out onto the ice.

Christian Horn was another guy on our team who always had a swagger. At one tournament in Duluth, Minnesota, we were trailing by a goal to the Minnesota Northern Wings early in the third period. My dad added some levity on the bench, telling Christian, "If you score on your next shift, I'll give you five dollars." Christian took on the challenge and smiled, "All right, I will." I played with Christian all the way up through high school, and he always had the ability to turn his game up another notch if he needed to. This moment was no exception. Christian went out and scored on his next shift and when he got back to the bench, he said, "Coach, you owe me five bucks." My dad grinned and happily paid him after the game.

After the first couple of Lightning summer seasons, the team began to turn over. It all started, it seemed, during the third period of a tournament game we played against the Minnesota Icemen, one of the other top summer AAA teams at the time. They would be another big rival as the years went on, but at this point, we were losing, 7–1, with about eight minutes to go. The game was over and we all knew it. Reid Trousdale, being a happy-go-lucky kid, started singing on the bench: "Bye Bye Bye" by NSYNC. The players on the bench who heard it started to laugh— and then were abruptly shut up when Coach Little heard it and lost it on him: "Are you singing? What are you doing? Show some pride, son! Unbelievable! Your game is over!"

A number of players were cut after this season, and I was very sad to see them dropped from the roster. Reid Trousdale, a true friend since I'd started playing hockey in Hanover, was gone, and as it turned out, we would never play together again. Also let go were Jack Goihl, a defenseman with an easygoing and positive attitude who was also a heck of a baseball player, and Miles Knutsen, who just loved to play hockey and, although he was relatively quiet in the locker room, always had a smile on his face. He could also hit a golf ball for miles, just like his name. Tony Cameranesi, one of the hardest-working players I ever skated with, left voluntarily to play for the Minnesota Icemen. He later went on to star at the University of Minnesota Duluth and was drafted into the NHL by the Toronto Maple Leafs.

The new players who came in had a much different attitude than the players who were cut. The earlier incarnation of the team had synergy and we all got along. We were a nice group of kids who had fun in our practices and games. We wanted to win, and most of the time did, but we didn't have that "win at any cost" mentality. However, this became the new team mantra going forward.

The new players Coach Williams brought in changed the culture in the locker room and on the bench. These additions included a couple kids who talked disrespectfully to other players—both on our team and the other teams—and even to parents. The locker room was no longer home to a tight, cohesive group. I did not mesh very well socially with this version of our team. This was partially my own fault; as a really quiet kid, I rarely socialized with teammates unless we had a team meal at a restaurant or pool party at a hotel.

When everyone in the locker room talked and joked around, I rarely participated. I just sat there, quietly minding my own business, following along just in case anyone said anything to me, in which case I'd give a one-word response just to get by. I was pretty much out of the loop because I didn't spend much time with my teammates away from the rink. They'd be talking about crude things they'd done during the week, and I didn't have anything to contribute to the conversation. I went to school, hung out with my school friends, did my homework, and played hockey. While my parents encouraged me to go socialize with my teammates, they also wanted me to be focused on my schoolwork. Looking back, I wish I had socialized more. I just didn't value relationships nearly as much as I do now; only my play on the ice mattered to me.

Overall, playing on this team could be described as a very challenging experience. Whipping-boy duty constantly brought me down mentally, so my confidence level was as low as the sewer by the end of each summer. Every year I tried to prove to the coaches I deserved to be on this team. I wanted their approval. I came to realize too late that this was a huge mistake. You can't force people to see you for who you are, especially when they have already decided they will never accept you.

I prevailed though, and the summer before high school hockey began, I participated in a lot of hockey camps, sometimes going to three different camps in one day. I stuck with these camps all throughout my high school years. My mom had to hire a driver to ferry me from rink to rink. My toughest days began with Karn Skating Dynamics at 7:00 a.m., followed by BSM's high school hockey summer training program, which was on and off ice for a couple hours total. From there I had a few hours off to catch my breath, and then I'd go for another off-ice workout as part of the Individual Skills Clinics hockey camp run by Rick Beckfeld and Pat O'Leary.

Beckfeld was involved with the USHL, and O'Leary won a national championship with the Gophers and played professionally. I was one of the youngest in the group, practicing alongside many who went on to play in college and the pros, and the camp really pushed me. I became much stronger off the ice and my shot especially improved. O'Leary would shoot with me all the time. I could never beat him playing P.I.G., but I got close a couple times. Even though I wasn't a top guy in his camp, he was willing to spend time with me because I put in the effort. I am very grateful to him.

To finish each night off, I had AAA Lightning summer team practice for an hour and a half. On nights with no AAA practice, I had soccer practice. To say I was exhausted by bedtime would be an understatement.

I hoped all this hard work would pay off as I headed into my first high school hockey season.

CHAPTER TWO

Red Knight Fever

I KNEW I WAS GOOD ENOUGH TO MAKE THE VARSITY TEAM IN MY FIRST season at Benilde-St. Margaret's. Good enough that I would catch the attention of college and pro scouts early on. Good enough to think I had a bright future in the game.

This small Catholic high school was one of the top ten for Minnesota hockey programs—no small feat—and the caliber of players on the squad was consistently high. The program turned out plenty of college and professional players, such as Troy Riddle and, most notably, Andrew Alberts, who played in the NHL for a decade. I planned on following in their footsteps.

Unfortunately, I was about to hit the wall of reality.

As an incoming sophomore to the BSM hockey program, I had been assured by Assistant Coach Adam Smith that I would make the varsity team and be no lower than the fourth defenseman in the rotation. Instead, I ended up on the junior varsity team. The three teammates I'd played with at Armstrong-Cooper a season earlier all made varsity. Two would go on to play Division I.

I came into the BSM program as a known quantity with a solid reputation as a player, and I'd been given the impression, based on conversations we had, that the coaches also felt the same way about me. But for some reason that all changed. Once in the program, I found the coaches to be inconsistent and deceptive, and the mind games they played extremely difficult to deal with.

Of the six spots in the lineup on the varsity defensive corps, the team returned three defensemen from the previous season, so there were three open spots for the taking. The fourth defenseman spot was handed to a less talented incoming freshman, and the remaining fifth and sixth spots went to upperclassmen, one of whom transferred in. For Coach Smith to tell me prior to the season that I would be a top-four defensemen on the team and then to be placed on JV even before the first skate, something fishy had to have transpired. At a top private school in the state, this wasn't out of the norm, which I recognized.

At practice the day before a game against Chisago Lakes, a program BSM usually manhandles, JV Coach Chris McGowan pulled me aside and said, "Hey Ryan, the varsity coaches told me you're going to be playing up with the varsity team tomorrow. They want to see what you can do, so be ready."

"Sounds good, coach." *It's about time*, I thought.

The next morning I went to school and scanned the roster posted by the gym, only to find my name listed not on the varsity game day roster but on JV.

A couple of days after playing in the JV game against Chisago Lakes, I met with Head Coach Craig Lumburgh and Assistant Coach Smith at the rink before my JV practice. I nervously asked, tail between my legs, "Hey, I wanted to ask, what do I need to do to improve and get playing time at varsity?"

After a couple seconds of thought, Craig Lumburgh replied, "Well, Ryan, you need to get in the gym and get stronger. We can't have defensemen at our level losing battles in the corners and need you to be strong on the puck."

"All right, got it," I said. "I can do that."

I took his words to heart and made it my number one priority to bulk up, all while watching Coaches Lumburgh and Smith play a couple of defensemen who hadn't made that same effort at varsity. I thought if I got bigger, there would be no way they couldn't play me.

In another game later in the season against St. Louis Park, Coach Smith informed me and another JV defenseman, Taylor Topousis, that we would be playing two periods of the JV game and two periods of the varsity game. The varsity team had one defenseman out for the game with an injury, and we were expected to once again steamroll our opponent, which allowed players like us to get a chance to play. We were listed on the varsity and JV rosters at school, so it seemed like the plan would be happening. To prep for the night ahead, Taylor and I went to his house after school to play an epic game of knee hockey. We made this a pre-game tradition, along with listening to the Notorious B.I.G. on the way to the game.

We made it through the first two periods of the JV game as planned, and then we were called into an empty open locker room by Adam Smith.

"Hey guys," he told us. "We are scratching our plan of bringing you guys up tonight, so just finish out the JV game."

Taylor and I looked at each other, perplexed, and he asked, "All right. Any reason for this?"

Coach Smith replied, "We just aren't going to do it. I don't need to give you an explanation."

"Okay, coach," I said.

Taylor and I walked back to the JV locker room pissed off.

"Why man, what do you think they're doing?" I asked.

All Taylor could say was, "No clue. This is so dumb, though."

We then proceeded to watch the varsity team play the game with five defensemen and one forward who moved back to take the sixth defenseman slot while we sat in the stands. Taylor and I could only shake our heads at the coaches' continued deception.

The one bright spot came at the end of the season, before section playoffs, when I had an opportunity to practice with the varsity team. I finally got to showcase my skills with the team, where I felt I should have been playing all season.

I remember one play specifically in which I made my presence felt, a play I hoped would open the coaches' eyes to realize what an opportunity they had missed by not putting me on varsity. As a player who was brought up just to practice, I skated on the scout team, helping to prepare the fourth-seeded varsity team to make it into the state tournament. The day before the big section 6AA semifinal matchup against top-seed Eden Prairie, I was playing on the penalty kill. Brett Patterson, a very creative and skilled forward who would later play Division I at Dartmouth, came through the middle of the ice, bringing the puck into the offensive zone with speed to set up the power play. Taking on the attitude of the indomitable title character from the movie *Rudy*, I treated my scout team duties as though I were playing for the Stanley Cup. I lined Patterson up at the blue line and flattened him, forcing him to the ice so violently his helmet flew off and skittered into the offensive zone corner. You don't see player's helmets flying off too often, so I knew I had clocked him pretty good. It was a clean hit.

The practice stopped, and Pat Borer, the team captain and a Niagara University commit at the time, skated over to me.

"What the hell are you doing?" he asked angrily.

I smiled and shook my head, "I don't know, man. He just ran into me."

Coach Lumburgh decided to switch to a new drill after that hit.

This single play solidified my belief that I had definitely belonged on the varsity team all season. The BSM varsity season ended the next day after the team lost to Eden Prairie. In my fantasy, I had hoped BSM would win that game and a defensive spot would miraculously come open for the section finale. Then I'd be given the chance to skate out on the ice at Mariucci Arena, home of the University of Minnesota Golden Gophers, and take my rightful place on the roster. Even if I didn't play, skating in warm-ups and freezing my butt off on the bench would at least raise my stock in the eyes of the girls at my high school.

Too bad it didn't happen.

That summer, I attended Rod Collins's three-week hockey camp in Bellingham, Washington. Collins was the general manager of the Wenatchee Wild, a junior team in the NAHL, and a former Shattuck-St. Mary's High School coach, so he was a big connection who could help me gain some credibility. We campers, many of whom went to Shattuck-St. Mary's, all stayed four to a room in the GuestHouse Inn near the arena. I shared a bed with John Draeger, a future Michigan State defenseman and eventual third-round pick by the NHL Minnesota Wild. He introduced me to the book called *Hockey Tough* by Saul Miller, which he seemed to treat as his bible while at the camp, reading it religiously every night. He was also a pretty mellow guy, so we got along very well and he proved to be a positive influence.

I put on 40 pounds of muscle that summer and now had a solid 180 pounds on my 6-foot-1 frame. The time and effort I put in that off-season was where I really developed my work ethic and discipline, and I am thankful to Pat O'Leary and Acceleration Northwest, where I trained much of the summer. I was in the weight room five days a week and on the ice multiple times a day, with barely any time to see my friends outside the rink. I drank protein shakes every night before bed to help pack on the pounds, throwing ice cream, milk, fruit, and protein powder into the blender—usually about thirty-two ounces and two thousand calories a shake. Crazy, but it worked.

I entered my junior season with an added sense of confidence and a bigger frame, and Coach Smith told me I would be slated as at least a top-four defenseman on the varsity team. I can't believe I fell for the same line I'd bit on before.

But once again, my season didn't go the way Coach Smith had convincingly pitched to me. I played on both the varsity and the JV teams throughout the season—essentially a swing player. I was a top-two defensemen based on ability but held the sixth or seventh spot in the varsity rotation. I typically played about three minutes per game, barely seeing the ice. I didn't even dress for section playoffs. During those section games, a group of girls at BSM made T-shirts with the varsity players' names on them and the saying: "My Knight in Shining Armor." (Our mascot was a red knight.) One of those girls wore a shirt with my name on it to a section playoff game—where I sat a few rows up from her in the stands. During the first period, she looked up and saw that not only was I not in the game, I was not even on the bench. I can't think of a time I felt more worthless and pathetic. What was worse, that game brought in a sellout crowd to the Bloomington Ice Gardens. If I had played, I would have gotten what I needed most—exposure.

Exposure puts you on the radar of college coaches and other influential people in the hockey world. Although I had played in select leagues and tournaments for years, the critical years to gain exposure to college, junior, and pro scouts is in high school. I was invisible to the high-level hockey personnel during those years because I didn't play.

And another hole in my hockey reality had become apparent: I didn't have many key connections. By this I mean I had no family ties or significant relationships with big-time local names in the college or pro ranks. And my parents—regular people with high ethical standards who were not born and raised in Minnesota—didn't suck up to coaches and throw money at them to gain preferential treatment. I'm not complaining about that; my parents set the bar high for doing the right thing, for which I am grateful. It's just that some other players had this kind of help.

I would describe my junior year as devastating for me. The coaches had deceived me for the second straight season. I bulked up like my coaches advised and was told before the season I would be a top-four defensemen in the rotation, but it didn't happen. I had no control over my playing time, even though I was a more skilled, smarter, and stronger player than most of my defensive teammates.

That season, BSM returned only two defensemen in the regular varsity rotation, so the third spot seemed like it had to be mine if I couldn't beat out one of the returnees. The third defenseman spot was handed to an incoming sophomore who was the brother of a senior defenseman on the team. The fourth spot was given to an incoming freshman who had little to no playing experience at the defensive position prior to joining the team. He was a forward playing defense. The remaining fifth and sixth spots were given to other upperclassmen I battled with. That Coach Smith had again told me before the season that I would be a top-four defenseman, and again I ended up on JV and varsity, was a crime and could not be explained by anyone logically. I learned that I couldn't dwell on things I have no control over. It is what it is.

Seniors on the team expressed surprise that I wasn't slotted to play on the first or second line throughout the year. I was at a loss as to how I could possibly reach my goal of playing Division I hockey.

In one game, the coaches slotted me to play the full JV game and one period of the varsity game. Late in the third period of the JV game we were winning, 6–1, I got whistled for a hooking penalty when the other team's forward grabbed my stick and dove on the ice, a common ploy to try and draw a penalty. When the JV game ended, Coach Smith stood outside the locker room waiting for me. He pulled me aside and explained, "Hey Ryan, we're not bringing you up tonight. We didn't like that you took a penalty in the third, and we won't reward you for that. You can get changed into your regular clothes. You're done for the night."

I held in my frustration and said, "All right." That seemingly harmless penalty call turned out to be harmful after all.

Coach Lumburgh always stared down his players who took penalties on their way to the penalty box, as if displaying his disgust would affect the offending player by letting them know they were now in the dog house. I and many others on the team found it more amusing. That was the image I had in my head as I took off my gear.

I felt sabotaged and started to think back to the comment Henry Porter had made to me when I was seven years old, promising I would never play high school hockey for him. Craig Lumburgh seemed to be following through with that plan on Porter's behalf.

Going into my senior year, I began to doubt my ability. The question that hounded me was this: How good was I, really? College good? Minor league good? Or maybe—eventually—NHL good? And if I really was a top-quality player, how would I ever reach my potential if I couldn't get the playing time I needed?

In the hockey world and at my age, there were several routes to a potentially successful future in hockey. At age seventeen, though, I wasn't mature enough to know for sure which path to choose, and I knew nothing about advisors and agents who help in this space. I felt like I had to find my way through a dizzying maze that had lots of routes and a very real chance of simply getting lost. There was an alphabet soup of potential leagues in which I could play: USHL, NAHL, BCHL, the list is endless. I had to ask myself, *Do I stay at BSM, where I will likely remain a reserve, or do I take another route to get more playing time and possibly more exposure?*

I had some decisions to make. I had several discussions with my parents, looking for their insight and guidance. They provided me with much needed clarity and suggestions but wanted the final decision to be my own.

And while I loved hockey, I had to consider another important component: I knew I wanted a solid college education to back me up if my hockey career petered out. If I chose to just play junior hockey for a couple of years after high school, I felt I would not be maximizing my full potential. All of my closest high school friends were going to college right after high school, and I wanted to have that same experience and become a well-rounded individual.

Depressing times set in during my junior season, to be sure—times when I thought all my effort counted for nothing. Sitting on the bench as the seventh defenseman in the rotation during a big game with plenty of scouts in the stands, not touching the ice until the last thirty seconds of a third-period win, and being a top defenseman in varsity practice all week and then not even getting to dress for the varsity game that week got me down mentally. But I just continued training and working hard, keeping my eye on the ultimate goal. I knew my talent was on par with top players on my team who went on to play Division I hockey, because I shut them all down in practices during my junior season. I knew I was good enough to play Division I hockey, but I lacked the exposure and connections to college coaches and scouts. Thankfully, there were ways in Minnesota to receive glimpses of exposure, such as junior team camps and the CCM Minnesota Hockey High Performance Model Camp that took most of the players who signed up early at the time, which I made sure to do.

In the spring before my senior year, I took part in the Wenatchee Wild NAHL junior camp in Prior Lake, Minnesota—the team run by Rod Collins, whom I had met the previous summer at his camp. The camp of nearly sixty players was put together for Wenatchee staff to evaluate players interested in playing for the team. The games were all open to the public, so scouts or coaches of high-level teams could attend. Collins offered me a spot on the roster after the camp in Prior Lake. The Wild were located fifteen hundred miles away in Wenatchee, Washington. I didn't really ponder this option very long because I valued my education at BSM. Picking up and moving to Washington to live with a billet family who would host and look after me for the year was not something I really wanted to do. Nevertheless, I was flattered by the offer and I fleetingly considered it.

Then the CCM Minnesota Hockey High Performance Model Camp—a weeklong hockey camp showcasing high school players in Minnesota—took place in June. I skated around Ridder Arena, home of the University of Minnesota women's team, along with dozens of other kids who had just completed their junior year of high school.

This is the opportunity you've been working for, I said to myself as I warmed up. Junior, Division III, and Division I college coaches from around the United States and Canada sat in the stands, there specifically to scout players like me. I had never seen so many college coaches at any of the games I'd played, so I understood what an opportunity I had been given to show off my skills. I spotted legendary Division I college coaches Don Lucia, Dean Blais, George Gwosdecky, Mike Eaves—all there sitting together—and so many other coaches, too, from colleges whose names I could not make out on their jackets.

Showtime.

A little before noon, I took the ice with my teammates. Because it was the first game of the day—in fact, the first game of the camp—anyone who mattered was there. Every team in the old Western Collegiate Hockey Association had either an assistant or a head coach sitting in the stands. Derek Schooley, the longtime head coach at Robert Morris, ran my team's bench.

I was in good company on the blue line, starting with defensemen Joe Schuldt, who would go on to play at Michigan Tech, and Ed Wittchow, who was drafted into the NHL by the Florida Panthers and went on to captain the University of Wisconsin. Looking back, being paired with these two, no doubt helped get the coaches' attention. I played a solid defensive game that day. As the weekend of games continued on, I put forth a strong, consistent effort in each game. All I hoped was that my play attracted the attention of at least one coach—just one person who could see what I had to offer. A few days later, I got an e-mail from one of those "other coaches" in the stands at the CCM Minnesota Hockey High Performance Model Camp:

Dear Ryan,

I hope the summer is treating you well. I had a chance to watch you at Model Camp, and I thought you were excellent. Coach Lumburgh had some great things to say about you as well. We are still looking for two defensemen for the 2011–12 season, and I hope to get out early in the season to watch you play. If you have any questions for me please don't hesitate to contact me. My cell is xxx-xxx-xxxx. Enjoy your summer and we will be in touch soon!

Thanks,
Ben Barr

The e-mail, trimmed with Union College garnet, made my spirits soar. It had always been my dream to play NCAA Division I college hockey. Now I had received some Division I interest, albeit from a school I really knew nothing about. I guessed the school had not performed well in its conference, the East Coast Athletic Conference, which doesn't get much coverage in the Midwest. And yet that little-known school in upstate New York would win a national championship a couple of years later.

Barr, who had attended Minnesota powerhouse prep school Shattuck-St. Mary's, was the Minnesota connection I felt I needed to play Division I. I responded the next day—but only after my father proofread my e-mail about twenty times. We then exchanged a few e-mails, which eventually led to phone conversations about recruitment and the prospect of playing junior hockey before college. Despite Union's original expression of interest in my coming in as a true freshman, the conversation morphed into something else: They wanted me to play two or possibly three years of junior hockey in a Tier II junior hockey league, such as the North American Hockey League, before I could come in and play for them. This was a common path to the Division I level, rather than going to college right after high school, so I didn't take the request as a big surprise.

I had not considered playing junior hockey, as I knew it would delay my jump to college. In junior hockey, players hope to develop enough skill to be eventually picked up by a college hockey program. By this time, I had a realistic approach to my hockey career. I wouldn't be seen as a top-end talent in high school since the probable playing time my senior year would again be limited, especially given the way I had been treated my first two years in the BSM program. My chances of playing in the professional ranks looked bleak. But still, I wanted to push my development as far as I could.

A local junior hockey option was the Minnesota Wildcats in the Minnesota Junior Hockey League—just minutes from my house. The Wildcats played in Maple Grove at the community center where I'd grown up skating with my family. The MNJHL drew many players who had been cut from their high school teams or players who just wouldn't give up their dream, even when they had little future in hockey. I knew that college coaches rarely attended these games to scout players. Only a few players from the league made it to the pros or Division I, though a handful played Division III each year.

Despite the dismal prospect of moving on, I saw playing in the MNJHL as a viable option to improve. The league played a roughly fifty-game schedule, which is double what the high school teams played. Most players were between eighteen and twenty years old, so I would also be playing with older, more mature players compared with high school hockey, where I would be the oldest and strongest. I knew that I would be a top-five player on this team, so there likely would be no concern about playing time. Most importantly, the Wildcats made it crystal clear that they wanted me to play for them.

As I looked forward to my senior year at BSM, Head Coach Craig Lumburgh told me I'd be the fourth or fifth defenseman in the rotation. Seniors could only be rostered and play on the varsity team. He planned to use me to strengthen and improve his incoming and inexperienced freshman players and would slot them ahead of me in varsity games. Typically, Craig Lumburgh played only the top four defensemen regularly. The fifth defenseman would see the ice for maybe six or seven shifts, and the sixth defenseman rarely saw the ice more than three shifts per game. Today I'd tell anyone in a similar position to bring a blanket and a book to the bench.

There were benefits to staying and playing at BSM as the role player I was now projected to be. I would be exposed to large crowds in the stands that included former players who relived their glory days each night. Because high school hockey in Minnesota is immensely popular, players enjoyed some social benefits as well. It seemed like every high school girl was smitten with a hockey player, although that hadn't really worked for me, unfortunately.

If I stayed, I'd get good-quality practice time against my skilled teammates, which was valuable in developing my skills. But I knew that if I didn't become one of the top-two defensemen in the coaching staff's lineup, I would not likely be watched by many scouts who attended our games.

That whole scenario contributed to an epiphany during the summer before my senior year: I didn't have to play at BSM—there were other options for me to consider, other teams I could play on while still attending BSM. What a concept. Local junior hockey was one of those options.

Leaving high school hockey early to play junior hockey is a hotly debated topic in Minnesota. There is no "right" path to the highest levels of hockey, and players who choose to stay in Minnesota high school or leave early for junior hockey are often criticized or praised for doing so. My decision to leave high school hockey sent shockwaves through the BSM hockey program: Because of its strong reputation and winning ways, while I was at BSM, I was the only player to voluntarily walk away from the varsity team. My parents fully supported and agreed with my decision. I felt relieved, even empowered that I would no longer be at the mercy of my high school hockey coaches or the political mess that seems to occur in high school sports. In making this decision, I realized how much stock I had put into my coaches' words, and after two years of taking to heart their words and opinions, they meant nothing to me anymore.

Although I planned to play in the MNJHL, I skated in the BSM tryouts, as I hadn't informed anyone of my decision yet. I wanted to see how I would be treated by the coaching staff and to show them on the ice what they'd be losing, if they needed a reminder. During the first two days of tryouts, a number of the varsity returning players sat up in the stands stuffing their faces full of food while I and a bunch of other players participated in the tryout. It was a joke and gave me a clear signal that I wasn't a relevant part of Craig Lumburgh's plan for the upcoming season. Just before the third day of tryouts, I walked through the long locker room hallway and into Coach Lumburgh's office. I spent all day at school trying to come up with what I would say to him, and I felt so anxious.

Shaking, I said, "Hey Coach, can I talk to you for a minute?"

"Hey Ryan, sure, what's up?"

I sat down at his desk and went into my spiel: "I have spent a lot of time thinking about this, and am going to leave your program. This summer has opened my eyes to other options where I can be a valued member of a team. I need to play and won't be able to do it here, so I must leave to keep developing my game. My time here these past couple of years hasn't gone anything like I hoped. I have to do what is best for my future."

Craig Lumburgh, taken back by my words responded, "Really, I'm shocked. You are a good player Ryan and you definitely provide us valuable depth and size on defense. Where are you planning to go?"

"I'm going to play in the Minnesota Junior League." I then started to choke up and continued, "Thanks for coaching me."

Craig Lumburgh didn't react, sitting there stunned and stone-faced, so I stood up and walked out of his office with tears starting down my face. But once I made it out of the locker room, the tears gave way to a big smile.

I had finally stood up for myself and believed in myself. I knew I was a top player who would never get the playing time I deserved. I knew the Minnesota Wildcats would value and enjoy having me on their roster. A small part of me wished I could tell Coach Lumburgh, "Have a great season lacking more than one competent defenseman while I tear it up elsewhere." Luckily, my better judgment prevailed.

BSM lost in the section semifinals once again that season, this time at the hands of Wayzata High School.

The difficult couple of years I played hockey at BSM, in a situation where I could control only my thoughts and actions but not my circumstances, were extremely mentally challenging and demoralizing. Life doesn't always work out how you envision it. My coaches' mind games might have broken my spirit more than a few times during my BSM High School hockey career, but they didn't drive me out—I left on my own terms. I made a choice to not allow their behavior to coerce me into abandoning my hockey dream. I would continue to keep moving my dream forward in spite of them.

CHAPTER THREE

Decisions, Decisions

THE DAY AFTER I LEFT THE BSM HOCKEY PROGRAM, CLASSMATES AND teammates alike pulled me aside. They couldn't fathom why I would choose to play in what they considered an inferior league instead on a top-ten team in the state. Nobody understood the decision but me, and I was content with that. I refused to follow the straight-and-narrow traditional Minnesota hockey path.

If I cared more about my peers' opinions, I would have taken the safe route—staying with BSM and playing out my role as decided by those coaches. However, I felt that my ultimate goal of developing into a Division I player depended on getting enough quality playing time, which would not happen if I stayed at BSM.

It was a risky move, to be sure—but ultimately the right one. When I started playing for the Wildcats, my hockey career began to take flight. The coaching staff of Jon Liesmaki, Cal Ballard, and Phil Diskerud gave me the much-needed freedom to grow and develop as a player. Most important, they were genuinely happy to have me on their team, and they saw potential in me. They fostered a culture that allowed players to make mistakes so we could learn and grow. That season I went on to lead all defensemen on the team in points and ranked second in total points overall. I finished second in the MNJHL in points as a defenseman. I was selected to the MNJHL All-Star team and played in the Tier III Junior National Tournament in Rochester, Minnesota.

But perhaps what made me proudest was my role on the Wildcat team—one of the go-to players in every game I played, something I had not experienced since my time in bantams. I became a leader and learned to take responsibility for how we fared in every game. The confidence my coaches and teammates had in me contributed to my development and maturity, both as a player and as a person. I will always be grateful to those coaches and team management.

And yet, the Minnesota Wildcats won only four games out of more than forty that season. Our record didn't reflect our effort, but mentally it was a struggle for many of the guys on my team. Most of my teammates were nineteen- and twenty-year-olds who were either going to community college or working. Outside of a couple who eventually went on to play Division III, the rest would end their careers in this league.

Even though I was a top player in the MNJHL, I knew that my hopes of going straight from high school to a Division I hockey team were virtually impossible. I would have to take the route that Ben Barr of Union College suggested to me: Play two or three years of junior hockey after high school, hoping I would get enough exposure to give myself a shot at a scholarship offer. I didn't want to do that because I wanted to go to college right away, and I never considered playing at the Division III level. I'd already played hockey at a small school. It was time for the big Division I school experience.

So, what were my options?

Really, I had only one in the United States: club hockey in the American Collegiate Hockey Association. The ACHA provides structure and regulations, sponsors national tournaments, and recognizes players through national awards. It has five divisions (three men's and two women's) with more than 450 teams around the United States. Teams do not offer athletic scholarships and typically receive far less university funding.

When I researched and applied to colleges, I knew nothing about club hockey in terms of the structure and the caliber of play. During my senior year, I received acceptance letters from Northeastern, Michigan State, Michigan Tech, and UMass, all of which admitted me directly into their engineering programs. Despite this, I eliminated these options and narrowed my options to Cornell University, Penn State, Rensselaer Polytechnic Institute, and the University of Washington. Each school offered me the opportunity to play ACHA hockey and get a strong education to prepare me for life in the real world, while all but UW had Division I programs I could try to walk onto.

Cornell became my dream school after I watched the Big Red take on the University of Minnesota in the 2005 NCAA Division I West Regional Final. My family had seats next to the Cornell Pep Band, and their small but enthusiastic following from Ithaca, New York, captured my attention. Their fans held up newspapers in front of their faces as if they were reading them to show disinterest in the Gophers starting lineup, and they chanted and cheered all game long. I marveled at the energy they brought to the arena and instantly fell in love with the school. I saw Cornell, an Ivy League school with a solid hockey program, as my goal.

I contacted the club hockey coaches at these schools, all of whom said that if I was accepted, they would talk to me. In my high school film studies class, my friends and I produced a short YouTube video called *Minkoff (Road to Cornell)*. That was the beginning of my acting career, and it ended later on when we made a part 2. I sent in my early decision application to Cornell—and then waited. To give myself a better chance, I applied to the school of music, citing my years of playing the saxophone in both junior and senior high school. I'd gladly keep my saxophone playing days alive if I were to be accepted. But even though I was a member of the National Honor Society and volunteered quite a bit throughout high school and in the community, I didn't have a 4.0 GPA or the necessary test scores to really give myself a legitimate shot at acceptance. As I feared, I received the dreaded rejection letter. Although I was not surprised by the result, I had still hoped for some kind of miracle. That dream was laid to rest.

Penn State became my second choice, which seemed like good timing as they were soon to announce the inception of a Division I hockey program. They already had a powerhouse club hockey team. I e-mailed and called their coaches, and we communicated back and forth. But once their focus turned solely to their future DI program, I stopped hearing from them. Looking back, I am glad I didn't go there, as I would have been a freshman during the Jerry Sandusky scandal and the ensuing chaos.

RPI, a small school known for its excellent engineering program, appealed to me, as that was the field I planned to study. I received a lot of information from the club head coach, Tim Cooley, who faithfully responded to my e-mails. He told me I'd have an opportunity to be a walk-on to their Division I team. The only downside, other than being situated in the industrial-looking city of Troy, New York, was that the student population consisted of only 30 percent females. That wouldn't work for me in college, especially since I had been pretty quiet socially in high school and desired a more favorable gender ratio. I needed a bigger pool if I planned on meeting the woman of my dreams, and RPI was not going to cut it.

That left the University of Washington. I applied the day before the application deadline. My mom had grown up in the nearby town of Mount Vernon, about sixty miles north of Seattle, and my grandparents still lived there. My parents gently suggested I apply, noting that it would be good to have a West Coast option and the possibility of some relatives nearby. UW had a club hockey team, but at the time I felt that since the school was on the West Coast, the team had to be of low quality.

Nevertheless, I found Head Coach David Kell, an Ohio native who had attended St. Mary's University in Minnesota, to be very informative and responsive. He put me in touch with Alex Wytaske, a Hastings, Minnesota, native on the team, who reached out to me to discuss life at UW. Alex told of the wonders of UDub (as it's known) and how much he enjoyed playing on the hockey team—which, of course, is exactly what I expected to hear. The day I received my acceptance letter from UW, Coach Kell called to congratulate me.

I researched the UW hockey team and found myself pleasantly surprised and encouraged that I'd be playing competitive hockey in a solid program. The team had just won the PAC-8 Conference (called PAC-8 because only eight teams in the PAC-12 conference participated in the league)—composed of Washington State University; the University of Oregon; the University of Utah; the University of California, Berkeley; UCLA; USC; Arizona State; and Stanford. Chris Stephenson, who was one of the assistant coaches, is the son of former Philadelphia Flyers goalie Wayne Stephenson. Chris had played hockey at Holy Cross

College, a Division I program. I saw the previous season's schedule had the team flying to Los Angeles as well as visiting other traditional Division I PAC-12 schools. I started thinking about the opportunity to travel, play hockey, and enjoy 80-degree weather at the beach on various road trips. The whole program started to sound pretty good to me.

This was countered by a bit more discouraging news. I examined the roster and saw that most players were from Washington, with a couple from Alaska and California—not exactly stereotypical hockey hotbeds like Minnesota and Massachusetts. Still, two players hailed from my home state and British Columbia, known for deep talent in hockey. Then I checked out the game and practice schedule. Games were played at 10:00 p.m., with practices at 11:00 p.m. during the week. Once again, doubts crept in. How could anyone take the program seriously if not only practices but also the games occurred so late at night?

And then came the final kicker: I had to pony up $2,000 to play. So much for being a poor college student.

After deliberating on the mixture of positives and negatives of the hockey programs and the schools, I decided to commit to the University of Washington. I set a goal of making this the best hockey experience possible for me at UW and pledged to help this team get to the highest level possible. I wanted to be the player who made a big difference in the program and put the team on the map.

Simply put, I wanted to be the best player to ever play at UW and in the ACHA.

The trek toward that goal began in the summer leading up to the start of college in the fall of 2011. Although I was relieved to finally know where I'd be attending college and playing hockey, an internal debate still raged inside me. Was I giving up on my dream of Division I hockey and settling for less? Or was I going to a school that provided me the opportunity to do something bigger and more impactful? I was feeling—at least at first—that all my hard work to play Division I had been for nothing, that I had settled for less when I accepted playing club hockey at UW.

My parents stepped in and helped me see that my dedication during my fourteen years playing hockey would pay off. In addition to my dad's success in college athletics, my mother had played softball and volleyball at Western Washington University. They had both dedicated a portion of their college life to their respective sports, so they knew how important playing was to me.

They stressed that I would be able to enjoy the full college experience while playing hockey, which ultimately is what I wanted. If I did well, I had to believe somebody would find me and see that I had the potential to go pro after college. At the very least, I wanted to try out for a minor-league hockey team after graduation—a reasonable goal. At the time there were more than fifty players from the ACHA who had played some form of hockey professionally; notably, Todd Orlando, a former ACHA player from Oakland University, had participated in the Philadelphia Flyers NHL training camp, and Lindenwood University ACHA player Daniel Walcott had been drafted by the New York Rangers.

As I prepared to head to UW, I thought that while I might not make it to an NHL training camp, I knew I would get to the professional level. I truly believed I could get just as far in the hockey world as those going the Division I hockey route, although others might have thought I was crazy to think so.

It's true that club hockey does not have the status and prestige of Division I. I knew I would not have people screaming my name. I knew I would not be walking around campus with my ten different team out-fits and sweet-looking uniforms, fellow students noticing and admiring me as I passed. But even leaving my Division I dream behind, I would achieve the self-satisfaction and confidence I needed to succeed.

The delicate art of tricking one's mind is a wonderful thing, one I had mastered by then. *Those Division I hockey players may be big shots now,* I thought to myself, *but I will surpass them during college and afterward in other areas of life—or maybe even in hockey too.* With these thoughts in mind, I looked forward with anticipation and excitement to my new life attending UW and playing ACHA hockey.

After my Minnesota Wildcats season ended in March, I began training at 1st Athlete, an athletic training program sought after by plenty of junior, Division III, Division I, and professional players. It is one of the premier training facilities for hockey in the state of

Minnesota and possibly in the entire United States. I trained five days a week on and off the ice with other players in my age group, all while being surrounded by NHLers such as Dustin Byfuglien, Erik Johnson, and various Minnesota Wild players. I sat low on the hockey totem pole at 1st Athlete, but the staff treated me just like the NHL guys in the room, on and off the ice.

By the time I finished training, I felt well prepared for my next hockey experience.

I arrived in Seattle in June for a three-day orientation to register for classes and take a campus tour. My father and I met Coach Kell at a coffee shop near campus. A paralegal who worked in downtown Seattle, Kell was in his mid-thirties and had been coaching the team since the early 2000s. Short and stocky with a full head of black hair and an impressively thick beard, Kell presented a somewhat intimidating persona. But he filled me with valuable information about where I'd be playing hockey for the next four years.

"The program is growing," he said, his enthusiasm evident, "slowly but steadily. Each season we have an increasing number of fans and a better pool of players."

He mentioned that Robby Maxwell, a UW player who graduated a couple years before I came in, had gone on to participate in a pro camp after graduating. I wasn't sure if I should believe him, having no way to tell what level of "pro camp" Maxwell attended. But it still assured me in some way that I could do the same after graduation if I wanted to.

The UW Pep Band played at the home games, he said with a certain pride, and that more than five hundred enthusiastic fans attended games against archrival University of Oregon. Coming from Minnesota, I didn't find five hundred people at a game to be very impressive, but at least it was more than a handful of family and friends.

Coach Kell invited me to play with the UW team in a men's league game the following day. Although I had brought my hockey gear with me to Seattle, I hesitated, a bit nervous because I didn't know what to expect. Would the players be okay with me just showing up and playing with them? How good were my future teammates? Would I be disappointed? Would they? My hubris didn't let me really consider the latter possibility.

A couple hours before the game, I went to Delfino's Pizza near the UW campus, where I gorged myself on a large pizza. I think I chose to eat so much—against my dad's advice—because this was just a summer game, and I tried to downplay in my head the upcoming meeting with my teammates. The truth is, I felt nervous.

It turned out the level of play was higher than I expected; I did not stand out and I certainly did not control the game. I ended up with a stomachache and actually played poorly compared to what I knew I could do. Lesson learned: Don't eat a 16-inch meat lover's pizza an hour and a half before game time.

By the end of the game, my lackluster play aside, I knew I could dominate if the level of play came close to what I had just seen. And despite what I felt was a dull performance, my future teammates welcomed me, and I took comfort in that.

After returning home, I continued training at 1st Athlete. Starting in late August, one by one all of my high school friends left for their respective universities. I had to wait until September 17, when I finally flew out to UW to begin my new adventure. My father came with me to help with the move into Haggett Hall, where I would share a tiny, octagon-shaped room with some random roommate. Saying goodbye to my dad, letting go of my family and living so far away, was difficult.

Toto, I'm not in Kansas anymore.

My roommate was a townie, a junior majoring in geography. He had grown up five minutes from campus. I had been hoping for someone in a situation close to mine, maybe a jock or just somebody from another state who had to adapt to being far from home. So much for that. He ended up keeping to himself for the most part, though we bonded over UW football and basketball. It didn't matter too much, as I had hockey and my new classes on my mind.

Tryouts began the next day. I felt the thrill of anticipation, excited to show what I could do. Going in, I had an idea of what I would find, but I wondered how the whole team would look, as this was a new season. Would other players be coming in as freshmen? How many players were returning? Coach Kell had told me he thought there would be six or seven new guys, but he didn't know for sure if any of them would play but me. Eighteen players showed up to tryouts, so we all knew—not that I was worried—that unless someone basically couldn't skate, everyone would most likely make the team. This was a new and different universe, to be sure, compared to the ultracompetitive environment I was accustomed to in Minnesota.

There were two other new players, both goalies. Jacob Gilmore, from the Tri-Cities area in Eastern Washington, had Western Hockey League interest while playing for the Seattle Totems, a Tier III Junior A team. He looked like a very promising goalie from the outset. The other was Casey Moore, who would be redshirting his freshman year. I didn't know you could redshirt in club hockey, but he did it. This meant most of the roster consisted of seasoned returning players from a team that had won the PAC-8 Conference.

The weeklong tryouts—which started at 10:30 each night at Olympicview Arena—gave me the chance to make a statement, and I made the most of that opportunity. From the start, everyone could see I was the most skilled player on the ice.

Olympicview, our home ice, was a fifteen-minute drive from campus, something of an inconvenience. Most schools I knew had their own rink on campus or nearby. However, carpooling allowed us to get to know each other. I rode with Jason Bartlett, a sophomore economics major from Federal Way, Washington. Two of his roommates—Michael Remedios, a sophomore law, societies, and justice major from San Francisco, California; and Andrew Johnson, a sophomore biomedical engineering student from Fairbanks, Alaska—rode with us. All three of them were welcoming, and we became good friends.

We played our first game of the season, an away exhibition, against my mom's alma mater, Western Washington University in Bellingham. Before the game, we got our white jerseys with HUSKIES in purple lettering and gold trim displayed on the chest; socks, some of which had holes in them from the previous season's usage; helmet stickers of the purple W; and, for those lucky enough to be at the head of the line as the team had only a few, UW breezer covers. When I played hockey in Minnesota, all of my teams had cool sweat suits and new uniforms and gear. At UW, I got a sweat suit jacket one size too large made by an off-brand company I had never heard of and an old, sweat-stained jersey with the number 83 on the back—one of the few jerseys available.

Stefan Sobiek, a recent graduate and one of the best players at UW the previous few years, had worn 83. I had planned on wearing number 3 at UW, in honor of my childhood idol, University of Minnesota star and former NHLer Jordan Leopold. Kell had told me earlier in the summer that the team had a number 3 jersey for me, but in reality, they didn't. However, the number 83 jersey had an "A" patch on it, since Stefan had been the assistant captain. So I appeared to be the assistant captain on the ice as a freshman in my first game.

Still, the lack of gear and UW-branded equipment and uniforms frustrated me. I wanted a new jersey, Bauer clothing, and discounts on gear, sticks, and other things. I wanted to look like a Division I hockey player on the ice. I wanted to look prestigious. I wanted people to be able to look at me outside the rink and know that I was on the UW hockey team. I understood that I was playing on a club team with enough money to barely cover ice bills and travel. But I knew we could do better. Getting new jerseys and clothing was the first thing I wanted to improve with the UW hockey team: Look good, play good, and command respect.

Apparently, WWU had a pretty good team, with the schools typically splitting the annual two-game series. They brought out a crowd of about a thousand fans to their home rink at the Bellingham Sportsplex, a pretty good turnout.

I wanted to get the season off to a winning start. It did not go as I planned.

Adapting to a new level of play, I played sluggishly—slow, uncomfortable, and lacking confidence. I gave up a breakaway and got caught out of position a number of times—overthinking and trying to do too much. I knew I was capable of controlling the game, but I didn't. One word describes my performance: awful. We ended up losing, 4–3.

The next week at practice, Coaches Stephenson and Kell, pointing to my skills and playmaking, suggested I play forward. I had hardly ever played up front in my career. I had hated forwards growing up. They never back-checked, were never open on breakouts, and never passed the puck back to me at the point. It was always the defensemen—never the forwards—who were blamed for the goals against. Now I would be the one cited for not getting back, not being open, and not passing to the defensemen.

Over the course of my defensive career, I had adapted my playing style. I started out as a stay-at-home defenseman. All I cared about was having a great plus/minus rating and getting assists. But because I saw how the defensemen at BSM who played up and on offense got the playing time, I changed my style and became aggressive and attacking—always trying to score. At UW, I greeted the idea that I play forward with skepticism. Soon enough, however, I realized this change would work best—not only for me, but for the team.

Having to fill Stefan's skates presented a big challenge. Coming into the season, I set a personal goal of leading the team and PAC-8 Conference in total points. It remained my goal regardless of what position I was playing. If I accomplished that, I thought, I'd be fulfilling my role on the team and helping to continue the Huskies' past couple years of success.

After two more exhibition games against Trinity Western University in British Columbia, we were ready to begin the regular season. Team president Bryce Johnson, a senior biomedical engineering student from the St. Louis area, had Coach Kell schedule our first games in St. Louis at the ACHA Showcase Tournament. Hosted by Lindenwood University, this was essentially Bryce's coming home party. We were scheduled to play Texas A&M, New Jersey Institute of Technology, and St. Louis University.

A buzz of excitement hummed through my body as we boarded the plane. I was ready to get off to a strong start in my college career.

PART TWO

DAWG DAZE

Introductions

As the beneficiary of many tap-in goals playing on Ryan's line for two and a half years at UW, I can honestly say I've never had more fun with hockey than I did in the games I skated alongside him. My first real interaction with Ryan came at the breakfast spot Denny's at around 3:00 a.m. in Las Vegas after playing a game at midnight. I had joined the team a couple of days prior and hadn't gotten to know anyone yet. We sat down with a couple other teammates and all asked for a round of waters to start. That water didn't come to our table for a half hour. What began as a joking matter of "Maybe the Denny's workers fell asleep" eventually turned into "What the heck is going on here—did all the staff go home?" We were eventually served and enjoyed a classic Denny's run. Looking back, this time spent joking around waiting for water in the middle of the night provided time for us to get to know each other. From then on, we developed some incredible chemistry. Ryan strived for excellence, and he really pushed me to be the best I could be. I am honored to call him a close friend.

—Alex Black
University of Washington Hockey (2012–2016)

We all knew Ryan was the best player on the ice at UW, but he'd never admit it. He was humble and treated every person in the locker room with respect. He had a tremendous calming presence as the captain and leader of our program. Entering college and playing as a freshman can be a stressful situation. You want to fit in with the guys when there is clearly a maturity difference. I will never forget how he always went out of his way to make the new guys like myself feel welcome no matter how small a role on the team we had, whether it be asking how we were doing or making sure we all were coming over for a team event—all done while perennially being one of the top scorers in the nation.

I could say a lot more, but I'll keep it short. Everything always comes back to how proud his friends, peers, and family always are of him. He is a tremendous role model within the community, has an entrepreneurial spirit that is inspirational to a lot of people, and a legacy within the UW and Seattle hockey community that will only continue to grow.

—Keenan Smith
University of Washington Hockey (2013–2017)

CHAPTER FOUR

Fresh Purple and Gold

COACH STEPHENSON PAID FOR OUR FLIGHTS TO ST. LOUIS, WHICH RAN about $5,000. He generously covered the cost because the team had no funds; most players hadn't paid their dues yet. The chances he would ever see that money again were slim to none, as we were all poor college kids.

My dad was at the tournament. Having him there to watch my first ACHA games meant everything to me—and to him. He didn't miss any of my games when I was growing up, and now that I played so far away for a team with no media coverage, he wouldn't be seeing very many. He had played a significant role in the development of my youth hockey career, priding himself on showing up to every game, being involved with and managing various teams, and running hockey websites. He loved being at my sporting events because he could give to me the attention and guidance he didn't get in his own youth. I knew missing these next few years of college hockey would be tough on him.

I found that weekend to be quite an introduction to club hockey. While most of us took an early morning flight from Sea-Tac Airport, about twenty minutes from campus, a few guys made it into St. Louis a day earlier. When we met up with them, we heard stories of an eventful evening where they were offered cocaine while staying at a sketchy hotel in a not-so-great neighborhood. (Our lack of funds impacted the choice of accommodations.)

With no team bus, we took three rental minivans to the Lindenwood University arena for our game at 9:15 p.m. against Texas A&M. We arrived about an hour before game time, all casually dressed in various

UW clothing, looking like slobs compared to the Aggies, who all wore suits and ties. Talk about showing up looking ready to go into battle. Five minutes before the game, while our upperclassmen complained about not being able to hit the St. Louis bar scene due to our game time, coach Kell came in the room.

"All right, boys," he said. "Let's get off to a good start this season. This is a big game for our regional hopes, so come out ready to play. Their goalie sucks, so get plenty of shots on net."

I scored the lone goal midway through the second period of a 5–1 loss, which wasn't pretty. A muffin of a shot between the goalie's legs off the draw from the left-wing circle is not how I expected my first ACHA goal to look. I played on a line with Jordan Chernesky, a Canadian, and Corey James, a native of Lynnwood, Washington. Making two consecutive tape-to-tape passes up the ice together was like tossing a bottle into the ocean and praying it would find its way to the intended recipient. We were out of sync all night. Our line did develop a bit of chemistry as the weekend went on, connecting on a couple of pretty passing plays in our victory over New Jersey Institute of Technology the next night, but then we went back to tossing bottles into the ocean and lost to St. Louis University on the last day. I enjoyed seeing my dad and spending some time with him sightseeing around St. Louis, seeing the Gateway Arch and Busch Stadium, but I'll admit to being disappointed that he didn't get to see us play very well.

I learned quickly that my teammates on this experienced veteran team went on road trips not for the games but for the travel destination. I understood that college kids like to have fun and party—and I was no exception. But I hadn't experienced playing on a team where the players didn't put winning the game as the number one priority. In high school, I'd spend all day in class thinking about playing a game that night—usually the only thing running through my mind, the typical Minnesota high school hockey player mentality. For the players on the UW team, the idea that we had a game to play seemed to come to them minutes before taking the ice. Most players on my team put their education at UW first and foremost, with partying a close second. I can't say I was used to that, either. On this road trip, many of my teammates went to the hotel lobby and coffee shop to do homework right up until we headed over to the rink. I didn't crack a textbook all trip, and neither did my line mate Corey James.

Corey grew up playing AAA hockey and attended various junior camps in the United States Hockey League and British Columbia Hockey League while in high school. Despite his solid ability, which could have landed him in a better program, UW was the only school he applied to and also happened to be fifteen minutes from his home. He grew up a die-hard UW fan, so he didn't consider applying anywhere else. If he hadn't been accepted, he would have played juniors somewhere. His build reminded me of a bowling ball—rock solid. He could run over opponents trying to knock him over on the ice, and if I hadn't known he played hockey, I might have mistaken him for an undersized fullback on the football team.

We started lifting together at the gym the following week. I thought I had a respectable build at 6-foot-2 and 195 pounds of mostly muscle, but he made me feel like a pipsqueak in the gym. I latched onto him, realizing he shared the same vision I did about playing hockey. He worked hard, he always had a smile on his face, and he kept things light—a great teammate.

Corey led a cheer at the end of our team warm-up before our home opener against Utah, one of the stronger teams in the league. Our pre-game ritual was a variation of what the UW Division I basketball team did before their games. We all crowded around Corey in a circle and started clapping, then sped that up and stomped our feet as fast as we could. He let out a yell and brought his hands up to his head, then back down. We imitated him then broke into jumping jacks while spelling out H-U-S-K-I-E-S; the climax of emotion moved us closer to him and had us jumping into each other, firing us up.

We were so fired up we swept the weekend series against Utah.

The following practice, Coach Kell pulled me aside: "Ryan, I'm going to tell you this just one time. Don't get sucked into the lazy, negative bullshit of some of these guys. You're better than that. You can change the attitude of the room."

I nodded. "You got it, Coach."

Funny how in tune he was with the team's vacation-like attitude. I took his advice and slowly saw positive changes to the level of my teammates' interest in their play. I changed somewhat, too, not feeling external pressure to perform like I did in high school or in juniors—only the pressure I put on myself. The environment of our team allowed me to relax, have no fear, and just go out and play.

Many club teams are not designed to be overly rigorous or demanding like a Division I team, so the team dynamic made sense. Club hockey is a way for those interested in playing organized hockey in college to come together and compete while still getting an education. Since no generous $100 million donation to UW—needed to build a Division I ice hockey program—had yet to be received, UW would remain at the club level.

We had no money for new jerseys, no money for warm-ups or decent apparel, no money to buy merchandise to sell, no money for a bus to get students to our games—no money for anything, it seemed. We would have to hold fundraisers and seek out team sponsors so we could change some of these dynamics. To my surprise, many of my teammates didn't want to put in the effort to do this, which points back to the reason our team had no funds to start the season.

I started to brainstorm ideas on my own. Why not find interns to get hands-on experience with business operations? That would take the burden off some of my teammates. Where else could we find resources to grow our hockey program? I didn't know but I felt determined to find out.

Our program had won the PAC-8 Conference title the previous season, so our fan base was at an all-time high. We would be losing a number of top-quality seniors at the end of the season, so I knew our window of opportunity to capitalize was now, before the team entered a rebuilding phase. This was the year to take the program to new heights, and that all started with keeping up the winning ways.

Every year we played four games against our archrival, the University of Oregon: the battle for the I-5 Cup, in honor of Interstate 5, the direct route between the two campuses. UW had won the I-5 Cup the past two seasons, so we were looking for the three-peat. Playing Oregon was the highlight of the season, as evidenced by everyone showing up to practice that week and nobody making up excuses about being sick or having schoolwork to take care of, like some tended to do. Both teams could lose every game during the season, but whichever team won the I-5 Cup considered theirs a successful season. Being new to the rivalry and not having grown up in the Pacific Northwest, I figured Washington State University would be our big-time rival. While UW hated WSU, we despised the University of Oregon even more.

To win the I-5 Cup, either one team had to win three out of the four games in the series, or, if each team won two games, a shootout following the fourth game would determine the winner. (Cue the shootout haters who don't like any game ending that way, let alone a series.)

The first two games of the I-5 Cup were played down in Eugene at the Rink Exchange near the Oregon campus. The pregame speech given by defenseman Bryce Johnson, who yelled, "F*** Oregon!" over and over, had everyone ready to roll. Once the games began, I quickly learned why we hated Oregon. The intensity reached a much higher level than any other game we had played up to that point. Players finished checks, players blocked shots, and always gave extra hacks on the wrists and the back of the legs—just like most games I played in high school and juniors.

We won the first game of the series, 3–1, in a hard-fought defensive battle. The second game, not so much. As the final minutes of the third period wound down, we were tied at five goals apiece. With just a few minutes left in the game, I got absolutely crushed by one of their players while receiving a pass through the neutral zone. I think I suffered a concussion, as I saw stars and my head began to throb, but I assured the coaches I was all right and kept playing. In the very last minute, we sustained pressure in the offensive zone, and I saw my chance. I dug up the puck out of a scrum near the right-wing hash marks. I initially fanned on a shot trying to throw it quickly toward the net. Then I attempted to shoot again, this time sending it fluttering through the goalie's legs and into the net. The "muffin man" strikes again.

The shot caught the goalie by surprise, and I know it's one he'd like to have back. We won, 6–5, off the biggest goal of my UW career so far.

As we left the ice, Bryce excitedly put his arm around me and exclaimed, "Ah, that's how you f*** Oregon. You're learning quickly."

Playing these games against Oregon and finally witnessing passion, effort, and focus displayed by my teammates, I got a glimpse of our true potential. Players didn't take off any shifts; everyone did their best and played with maximum effort. I felt reassured that my teammates did in fact love to play the game.

The following week, I started to act on my brilliant brainstorming of ways to improve this program. I came up with the idea of trying to have UW hockey T-shirts sold in the campus bookstore. Everyone who goes to or visits the school has to venture into the bookstore at one point or another, to buy textbooks or supplies or maybe a gift. I figured that could be the first step in cultivating awareness about our team.

I approached one of the store managers and gave her what I hoped was a winning smile. I introduced myself as the UW hockey team assistant captain.

"If we made some UW hockey T-shirts," I asked, "could you sell them and let us use the profits as a team fundraiser?"

But she immediately shook her head. "Nope. We aren't allowed to sell shirts that you make, let alone give you a cut of any shirts we'd have made if we were to do so. Of course, we often order new products to sell in the bookstore, but we need a reason. I haven't heard of any interest in buying UW hockey apparel—until you today. If there's some consistent interest, we could probably stock an item."

I took down her name and phone number and left, one thought in my mind: *I'll show her consistent interest.*

My genius plan was to call the store manager every couple of weeks, alter my voice, and ask if they sold UW hockey clothing. Then I'd go into the store twice a week and ask the clerks where I could find hockey apparel. When told they didn't carry anything, I'd act surprised, ask why, and suggest they should. My *Road to Cornell* acting skills were back on display.

On my next trip to the bookstore, I went straight to the checkout clerk and asked, "Do you have any UW hockey stuff? Like T-shirts or jerseys?"

The clerk looked at me in amazement. "Hockey? I didn't know we had a hockey team. We have a hockey team?"

"Yep," I said politely. "In fact, UW has had a hockey team since the 1920s."

She thought a moment, then said, "If we have anything it would probably be a T-shirt over in the team area." We walked together over to that section, but of course we spotted no hockey T-shirts.

"Let me go ask our manager why we don't have hockey T-shirts," she offered. But when she returned a few minutes later, she gave me an apologetic look.

"I guess nobody ever asks to purchase hockey shirts, so we don't carry any."

Just what I expected to hear. So far, so good on my plan of attack.

To finish the first half of the season, we headed to Colorado to play four non-conference games against four different schools. In our first game we faced Colorado State University in Fort Collins. Most of us were staying four to a room, sharing beds at the Holiday Inn in Boulder near the University of Colorado campus, about an hour away from CSU. But five others stayed at a family member's house—another new concept for me. Our coach approved this, so I assumed it must be a customary practice in club hockey.

When we arrived to play Colorado State, I had my first inkling that the fab five seniors not staying with us were in full tourist mode: None of them were there. I figured they wouldn't arrive at the arena an hour ahead of time, but I didn't think they would actually miss the start of the game. I was shocked that when they didn't make it for warm-ups, our coach remained unconcerned. All of the players at the arena speculated about what happened to them—from passed out drunk to stuck on the side of the road to dead in a ditch.

We had only two lines of forwards and three defensemen at the opening draw instead of three lines of forwards and five defensemen. CSU capitalized on this by scoring two quick goals right off the bat. The delinquents made a grand entrance halfway through the first period between whistles, waddling onto the ice, laughing and joking as if it was a Sunday skate in the off-season. As much as I wanted to chirp at them, I knew that if I did, I would be in for a hell of a time at the next hockey house party—though I probably would be anyway.

In an effort to maintain harmony on the bench, I kept my mouth shut; unfortunately, some of my teammates did not. They couldn't help yelling at the latecomers, which took all the focus away from the game. I thought we would be able to catch up and win the game after they arrived, but instead, we suffered a 7–2 blowout loss. We never did get the story behind their late arrival.

We followed up that horror show with an even worse blowout loss—this time at the hands of the University of Nevada, Las Vegas, 9–1. Nobody focused on the game, distracted by the dramatic Flatirons we stared at through the panoramic windows at the University of Colorado's arena. Usually the girls in the stands were what sidetracked our attention midgame, but those mountains—so close you could almost touch them—did their part.

One of our assistant coaches, Rob Ramsburgh, was filling in for Coaches Kell and Stephenson, who were unable to make the trip. In the locker room after the game, he absolutely ate us alive: "Why even show up to the next game if you're going to give such an embarrassing effort? Just catch your flight home now. I don't want to coach a team like this."

Nobody could disagree with his remarks.

We put up a fight against the University of Colorado Boulder squad the following night but again lost, 8–4, in front of a raucous crowd. This time we had the distraction of both CU's female fans in the stands and the view out the window, so we stood little chance. Afterward, we walked around the campus and then drove past all the raucous frats and sororities before heading to our hotel.

"This campus is sick," I said to Andrew Johnson. "Unreal girls, better hockey team, and a cool rink. Why didn't we go here?"

If I had visited here in high school, I might have been swayed after this trip. (Ironically, my sister attended CU and also played hockey there.)

Rounding out the road trip, we took another loss, this time to Arizona State University, 5–1. It was a less-than-stellar performance, going 0–4 on the road trip and losing pretty handily each game. That weekend on the ice in Colorado is one I wanted to forget. At least we had a fun vacation outside of the rink, hanging around the college-oriented town and hiking in the mountains above Boulder.

Before heading back home to Minnesota for winter break, I went to a party at our seniors' hockey house, the last one we would have for a month. I had begun to be pretty comfortable around most of my teammates, enjoying the camaraderie among the guys and showing up to all of the parties they invited me to after games. This was something I didn't do much with my teammates in high school, and I really liked the sense of community I felt on the team. I would be spending four years at UW, longer than any association I played with in my entire youth, so I figured I should enjoy it.

I hoped I might meet a lucky lady that night: Actually, I'll rephrase that—I hoped I would get lucky. So far, my interaction with any females at our hockey parties this season had been while intoxicated. The later the party went into the night, the more drinks my teammates would pour into me and the more talkative I got. I typically played beer pong and hung out with my teammates all night.

I thrived at the sorority "toast bar," which I looked forward to the most. When sorority girls headed back to their house from our parties, a few teammates would walk with them, and they were kind enough to let me tag along. It gave me the chance to venture into sorority houses—places I otherwise would never see the inside of—and mingle. "Mingle" might be a bit of a stretch, but I was surrounded by women who made sure I got something to eat: usually toast (hence the name), maybe some ramen, yogurt, or whatever else they had available. I didn't care. Free food and lots of friendly women—not a bad situation.

This night would likely end up no different than the others. But still, as a naive freshman just learning how to interact socially, I loved it all.

After Christmas break, I followed up on my scheme to get the bookstore to stock UW hockey T-shirts. Since starting my quest six weeks earlier, I had visited the store and made several phone calls to ask if the store had hockey T-shirts in stock. I placed a call to the UW bookstore manager, identifying myself as the young man who had originally spoken with her about stocking the shirts.

"I was wondering—have you received any more interest in UW hockey T-shirts?"

"As a matter of fact, I have," she said with surprise in her voice. "We've had phone calls and quite a few in-store requests, so I think we'll go ahead and print the shirts. I will put in an order later today, and I'd guess they'll be in the store by the end of the month."

My plan had worked.

"I can't thank you enough. You won't regret it," I assured her. "They will sell out once everyone finds out you've got them in stock. I'll make sure of that." Feeling magnanimous, I added, "And since you've never been to a UW hockey game, I'll bring you tickets for the rest of the season."

I wondered if she had just gotten sick of hearing from me and decided to give into my persistence. Still, I felt pretty proud of myself. How had no one thought about doing this before?

With great pride, and a huge grin on my face, I announced the news at practice that night.

"Nice work, bud," chirped Andrew Johnson. "Are you going to account for all five of their sales for the year?"

"Did you get your name and number printed on the back too?" asked Jordan Chernesky.

My teammates had a field day making fun of my enthusiasm. I didn't care. One task was accomplished, but there were many more to go.

The following weekend we met UCLA. If we swept the home series, we'd have the number one seed locked up going into the PAC-8 tournament. After a win in the first game, 3–1, I couldn't help but feel confident going into Saturday night's game—so confident I managed to score four goals in the first ten minutes of the game.

Four goals on four shifts. Once I had my hat trick, the sparse but enthusiastic crowd chanted, "MIN-KOFF! MIN-KOFF! MIN-KOFF!" whenever I had the puck and then when I came off the ice after the first period. I raised my right arm and pointed to the crowd after each goal. I hadn't experienced that kind of adoration ever before—except in my own mind as an eight-year-old kid playing mini sticks. I think it must have gone to my head, since I didn't get another point the rest of the game. Winning 8–3, we clinched a first-place finish in the league.

On Senior Weekend, Oregon would be coming up I-5 for the final two games of the season series. I planned to put on a good show. The number of students coming to our games had probably doubled since the start of the season, largely due to BYOB. If BYOB defines the typical college party, then our club hockey games could be seen as gigantic parties. We advertised to students and fans that they could bring alcohol into our games and drink whatever they wanted all night long. Olympicview didn't sell beer, nor, to my knowledge, did it even have a liquor license. I put up a ton of posters around campus to promote the Oregon matchup and even scrawled chalk signs on the main campus pathways, praying that rain didn't wash them away.

Students entered Olympicview Arena with brown bags and cases of beer. Once the word got out, we had around five hundred rowdy fans at both games. Even though the arena could have held twice as many people, that was our best home crowd of the season by far. Our unruliest fans sat close to the penalty box and relentlessly taunted the Oregon players during their penalties, upsetting a few Ducks to the point that some of them mouthed off to our fans—then got kicked out of the game for unsportsmanlike conduct. BYOB came up big for us there. As for the games, we were not going to lose to Oregon. We were too focused and, quite frankly, too good at home. We swept them in two hard-fought games, 4–1 and 3–2.

Spirits were at an all-time high among the guys on our way to play the final weekend of the regular season against the University of Utah in Salt Lake City and Utah State in Logan. Our road trip did not go too well for the "tourists," thanks to the availability of 3.2 percent beer and everything remotely entertaining closing at midnight. We lost to Utah, and then headed to face the Aggies of Utah State, a top-ranked team in the region and an acknowledged ACHA powerhouse that made the national tournament almost every year.

An electric atmosphere greeted us at Utah State, with a packed house of a couple thousand fans. The team had the setup I dreamed of: a rink near campus, a large student following, games streamed online with play-by-play, the team's own designated locker room, and players who were committed to improving their play. It was the closest I had seen an ACHA team look to a NCAA DI or DIII program from the outside.

The PA announcer read our lineup before the start of the game, with me starting at left wing. The goalie and other four skaters were all from Washington, and I was introduced as hailing from Minnesota. Each player in Utah State's starting lineup, however, came from Canada, the East Coast, or the Midwest. I laughed to myself, standing there on the blue line, knowing that I fit in on their roster better than my own.

We knew going into this game that it would be tough sledding. I had hoped we'd keep it close, but we didn't even put up a fight, losing 13–2— a fitting end to our road woes of the regular season.

Still, I won't forget the goal I scored on the power play in the middle of the second period. We were getting manhandled, 5-to-zip. I received a pass on the red line near the right-wing boards. The puck slid a bit off of my stick in front of me, causing the defenseman to try to poke it away. He missed, and I slipped past him, moving the puck through his legs. Bad look for that guy. I cut inside of the next defender and came up one-on-one with the goalie. Dipping my shoulder to fake a forehand shot, I moved the puck to the backhand and roofed it into the top left corner of the net.

I celebrated by sliding on one knee up the boards, pumping my fist from the goal line nearly all the way to the blue line. Classy move while getting smoked. Boos and the typical "scoreboard" chant—the fans' way of pointing out we were still getting beat—rained down from the crowd, bringing a smile to my face for a minute. I felt I belonged on the ice against the power of Utah State, but boy was I happy when the misery ended.

Playing this game not only showed me I could reach my potential with UW hockey, but really motivated me to keep improving both my play and the program, on and off the ice.

On the ice, we functioned as two different teams. At home, we were unbeatable, boasting a 13–0 record at Olympicview Arena. Playing at home—boosted by our supportive, rambunctious crowds who annoyed all our opponents—made us feel invincible. And the home crowds grew in numbers as the season went on. We took this aura of confidence into the locker room, knowing we were going to win before we stepped on the ice. Often, we sleepwalked through the first two periods, keeping the score close. It almost seemed as though we did that by design, a way to make sure fans stayed tuned into the game and didn't leave at midnight to go party instead of staying until the end. Then we'd turn on the switch for the third period—time to impress the ladies in the stands (if there were any)—and we would dominate. It sounds cocky, but we were good enough at this level that if we kept the game close going into the third, we knew we would get the "W." I had never been on a team before that could flip the switch like that.

Our games on the road told a different story, with a 6–10 record away from Olympicview. We could factor into our road struggles that we faced tough competition. All of the strong teams we played, we played on the road. Those discouraging results may have been different had we played at home. All four of the teams we played in Colorado were ranked in the top ten, as were Utah, Utah State, and St. Louis University. We hoped that despite all the losses to stronger teams, the strength of the competition in our schedule would benefit us in the final regional rankings. We needed to finish in the top ten to make the West Regionals.

We headed into the PAC-8 Conference Tournament as the number one seed, with a 12–2 conference record. We were lucky enough to be hosting the tournament, a huge advantage. Utah finished second in the league, followed by USC and UCLA. Only the top four teams made the PAC-8 Conference Tournament in the single-elimination playoff format the league used that season. We faced off against fourth-seed UCLA, while Utah took on USC. Like the previous series against UCLA, we took them out pretty easily, winning 7–2 in front of a packed house. Utah defeated USC in a shootout in the other semifinal to advance to the championship game. The anticipated showdown was set.

My dad flew out to Seattle to watch us play, making the tournament even more special for me. I had missed scanning the crowd and finding my dad sitting in the stands. Just feeling his presence at the rink elevated my spirits.

Going into the championship game, we were ranked twelfth in the region. The final rankings would be released after this game against Utah, so we were constantly bubble watching. Ranked sixth in the region, Utah was a pretty safe bet to qualify for West Regionals regardless of the outcome of the championship game. If we knocked them off to win the conference, we would have a good shot of nabbing the tenth and final spot, depending on other teams' results.

Each team played the final as though nobody wanted to make a mistake. Intense but boring to watch, it was dump-and-chase hockey all night. In the first period, Daniel Carson, a senior from Anchorage, Alaska, scored our first goal of the game on a harmless dump-in attempt. He fired the puck from between the red line and offensive blue line on target, going under the netminder's right arm and in. The goalie was obviously caught off guard by the shot, and the puck's waffling through the air probably made it tougher for him to pick up. It turned out to be the only goal we needed. In the final minute of the game, my line mate Corey James added an empty netter from center ice to secure the victory. Behind Danny Dougan's stellar performance in the net, we won the title with a shutout, 2–0.

"How about that! Way to battle tonight, boys! We set our sights on our goals this season and we hit 'em. Proud of you guys!" a sappy Coach Kell exclaimed.

Following the game, all four teams attended the PAC-8 Conference banquet in downtown Seattle. After we all enjoyed a delicious and collegial meal, the Pac-8 officials handed out coach and player awards based on the nominations and votes of all PAC-8 coaches.

Our very own Coach Kell won the Coach of the Year Award, and five players won awards: Daniel Carson, Bryce Johnson, and I made the second team, while Corey James and Danny Dougan made the first team.

There were a couple surprises here. The first was that Bryce made the second team. Our whole squad, including Bryce, at first sat in shocked silence when the commissioner announced his name. When Bryce jumped up and started laughing, we all broke into surprised applause. We had no idea how he could possibly win this award, as he had scored more goals in our own net (three) than in our opponents' (one) that year. We guessed Coach Kell must have nominated him, but still—how did he get enough votes from coaches around the league to win? I do know that all the work he put in to run our team during the season made him more than deserving of something.

The other surprise was that I didn't make the first team. I led the PAC-8 in points, and I thought that alone would have guaranteed me a spot. It made me think back to my days of getting screwed by the governing body of Buffalo hockey in squirts. Although I was still honored to win an award, I knew I would carry that first team snub with me into the next season.

Deservedly, Corey made the first team, as he'd had a breakout year in scoring. Over the course of the season, we had developed into a dangerous tandem: I would get him the puck and he would bury it. Danny had proved to be the best goalie in the league, so if he hadn't made the first team, it would have been a crime.

We had to wait until the next day to find out if our season would continue. After our solid victory, we felt we'd definitely qualified for regionals. Finally, Coach Kell posted the rankings in our Facebook group. We had jumped two spots, over both Denver and Texas A&M, to get the tenth and final seed in the West Regionals. We secured that last spot solely on the strength of our schedule. Every team we played that qualified for regionals had destroyed us, except for Utah. But despite those losses, we were rewarded for playing the tough games and playing them on the road.

As great as it was to make regionals for the first time in the program's roughly ninety-year history, the club had no money in the bank account to physically get there. West Regionals were set to take place in San Jose, California, so we would realistically need to fly there. (At least I hoped not to carpool!) Regionals started in two weeks, and since we hadn't anticipated making an appearance, no flights or hotels had been booked. It was going to cost around $8,000 for us to attend, and we had done virtually no substantial fundraising all season.

That meant we needed to come up with the funds quickly. We asked family members for donations, either personally or perhaps from the company where they worked. Bryce set up a UW Ice Hockey Fund through the UW Alumni Association with the help of UW Student Life's George Zeno. Without UW Student Life's help, we would never have raised enough money. Student Life agreed to match whatever funds we raised, which ended up being just about four grand.

We were headed to San Jose.

I will never be able to thank Bryce enough for the work he did in helping raise money, and for just being "El Presidente," as he referred to himself. Having to handle the finances, book trips, and just deal with all the challenges some of my teammates had presented throughout the season, he proved how he could get things done. I could see how fuming mad he got at times, caring about the program as much as I did. He would do anything for the team, on and off the ice.

I eventually wanted his job as president so I could make my mark on the club. Dan Herda, a junior forward from Bellingham, Washington, had already been chosen as the president-elect. He cared about the team and had helped Bryce out during the season, so he was a logical choice. I planned to take over for him after he graduated the following year.

Regionals used a single-elimination format, so if we lost, our season would be over. If we won, then we'd play one more game for a shot at making nationals. The top two teams in each regional ranking receive an automatic bid to the national tournament. Regionals are then used to send two more teams to the national tournament from each of the four regions. Eight teams traveled to San Jose, each vying for two spots in the national tournament, which consisted of sixteen teams total.

We were set to face off against a familiar foe, third seed Colorado State.

We kept it close for the majority of the game before losing, 7–3. Danny Dougan suffered an injury during the game that forced our backup goalie, Jacob Gilmore, to come into the game in the second period, when we were down only 2–1. Danny's injury came at the worst possible time in the game, while Colorado State was on a five-on-three power play.

Still, the experience of playing in the regional tournament felt special, as we accomplished a feat that no other UW hockey team had ever done. After the loss, I ended the weekend on a personal high note, making my first strip club appearance—in the audience, not on stage—in San Jose at a place called the Pink Panther with a few of my teammates. I sat back and took in the sights.

I knew I was going to miss the graduating seniors. No more Danny Dougan standing on his head to win us games. No more Tristan Wickliff, one of my favorite players, although I didn't get much time on the ice with him. He rarely showed up to practice and could crush me in FIFA on Xbox any day of the week. The other Tristan on the team, last name Vandermeer, would be missed for being a fatherly figure at the tender age of twenty-six. He loved being a part of the team. I could say the same thing about Nelson Beazley. Even he would admit that he was the least talented player on the team with not much playing experience, yet he still showed up to every practice and game. I admired that about him. We would also lose Erik Pearson, a defenseman who seemed to study Wikipedia articles more than his economics homework—an entertaining guy to be around, the king of obscure facts, whom I enjoyed getting to know. An unfortunate blow to the team came when Jeff McClintock left the team. At one time he had entertained an offer to play hockey at the Air Force Academy, but he suffered too many concussions, which ended his career. He was a solid defenseman and an even nicer guy to hang around with. He would be sorely missed.

The player I would miss the most was Alex Wytaske—a great guy, a Navy guy. You knew that the minute you met him: crew cut, perfect posture, a way of walking with confidence but not arrogance. Everyone respected him. When something needed to be done, Alex got it done. On the ice, he gave 100 percent, never letting his limited skill keep him down. He watched out for me during my first season on the team. Not only did I look up to Alex, I wanted to model my character after his.

As we moved into the spring quarter, I began to shift my focus to the next season. My goals were to not only lead the team and the conference again in points, but to break the team's record for total points in a season: 84, set by Brett Lawrence in 2002. I knew I could do it. I also wanted to win the PAC-8 first team award and to be an All-American in the

West Region, an honor awarded by the ACHA. Following the end of my sophomore season, the ACHA would put on an all-star tournament to which each ACHA conference sent a team to compete. I wanted the opportunity to play on that team.

I was officially made the vice president under new president Daniel Herda, to start the next season. One great thing about a club-run sport is that no one told me what I had to help with and what I could or couldn't do. So the first item on my agenda was to recruit Ice Girls for next season. What better way to solve my abysmal social game than to get a bunch of attractive girls in front of our fans at home games. I had heard about Ice Girls performing at USC, so I figured why not try here?

I made a "Wanted" poster to hang up in a few spots around campus. I got one inquiry from a freshman girl, but unfortunately, she never responded to my reply. Bryce suggested I bring the posters to the hockey house parties, where they were plastered up on the walls. The jokes thrown my way for pursuing my Ice Girls idea were never-ending, probably rightfully so.

Next, I looked into trying to get our games televised on UWTV, the University of Washington cable channel that reached many viewers in the state and could be accessed online. This was an impossible dream, considering it would cost about two grand per game. I would have to settle for a rental video camera from the UW communications department and then find some student to figure out how to stream it online for little to no cost from a rink with an awful internet connection.

I tabled both ideas and moved my focus to working on my anemic social life—meaning my lack of female companionship. I royally screwed up a potential relationship with a girl I met at a party held at the team's hockey house. When we initially met, we were fairly inebriated. She spotted me and decided to come over and tend to my poor soul, funneling water down my throat while I sat on some rickety stairs, all while my teammates ripped on her for helping me out.

I wanted to pursue her but found myself in unfamiliar territory, being naive and lacking any legitimate experience interacting with girls. We hung out a couple more times at parties and in dorm rooms, but after a few weeks, she sent me a message asking if I ever wanted to hang out more when we weren't drunk. We had only done that one time, playing board games with a few friends. I didn't know what to do or say, but for some reason I wasn't ready for a real, committed relationship. Needless to say, this ship sailed away.

Coming into UW, I had no friends or contacts in Seattle and no real experience with dating. Because I was often gone on weekends for late hockey games, I typically was not around on Friday and Saturday nights to party until really late at night. By then everyone was already plastered, and the night would be nothing more than a blurry memory. As a result, I didn't make too many friends with people outside of the team. Even if I did connect with someone and sent a text the next day to someone I'd met at 3:30 a.m., I often got no response or the "Who is this?" text, to which I would reply and then not hear back.

And although I had some family in the state of Washington, I really had no awareness of my surroundings in the city of Seattle. It took me my whole freshman year to figure out the lay of the land around the U District (so named because UW is located there). You could say I was kind of lost that first year and trying to find my way around on multiple fronts.

To make up for my less-than-stellar social life, I made the Dean's List for the spring quarter. That made me proud.

Before I went home to Minnesota for the summer, a few of my teammates and I flew down to San Francisco to run a concession stand at the US Open golf tournament to fundraise for our hockey team. Not only did we have a great time, we saw quality golf and raised more than $6,000. We stayed at Mikey Remedios parents' home in the hills of San Francisco and put in twelve-hour days on the course—from about 6:00 a.m. to 6:00 p.m.—for the week.

Since the practice rounds didn't bring in a lot of spectators to our concession stand the first couple days, we were able to follow a bunch of the stars, including Tiger Woods. We had plenty of fun working— maybe too much fun. Some of my teammates' frat brothers came down to help us out, and they pranked customers, doing things like splitting a hot dog and leaving only half of it in the bun. One guy split a hot dog in half but threw in half a banana to fill the rest of the bun. That really pissed off the customer when he opened the wrapped hot dog to put on the condiments, and we heard about it. Of course, we always gave these customers new hot dogs, although they were more than a little upset about standing in line for fifteen minutes only to be messed with by some smart-ass college kids. Still, the occasional prank did spice up the job.

We'd start drinking on the job at 10:00 a.m. sharp, the earliest the course was allowed to serve alcohol. By the afternoon we were in prime form. An unreal perk of working the concession stand was that we could fill our coffee cups every once in a while with the various beers served, usually an IPA or Lagunitas Little Sumpin' Sumpin'.

After the golf tournament, I headed back to Minnesota, looking forward to spending the summer at home, hanging out with some of my high school friends, and playing hockey at 1st Athlete again. I added work to that agenda, as I was trying to pay for school instead of relying on loans and my parents' support. I needed as much money as I could get.

My first week back, I started bright and early at 1st Athlete, spending time in the gym and on the ice from 7:30 to 11:30 a.m. After that I had roughly a five-hour break to eat and nap before heading to Amerilab Technologies, where I worked from 4:30 p.m. to 2:30 a.m. on an assembly line, packaging pills and prepping them to ship. One of my mom's day-care parents worked in management at the company and had helped me get the job. This was my first real job, as I had previously worked only for my mom at the preschool and daycare she ran out of my family's home.

One day in, I'd already had enough. The people I worked with could barely speak English, so I had no one to talk to the entire shift. My fingers felt like they were going to fall off from stuffing pills into bottles, and my feet hurt from standing on an unforgiving cement floor all night. One positive was that I gained a lot of respect for people who can do this type of work.

I lasted three weeks at Amerilab Technologies, but only because it took me two weeks and six days to find a new job that paid me the same wage of $12 an hour.

I picked up a new job thanks to Tanner Speltz, one of my best friends from high school. Tanner worked part-time running paper through a slitting machine at an advertising company owned by his father, Joe, that produced large-print ads you might see on semitrucks or at gas stations.

I started running the paper-slitting machine from 12:00 to 8:00 p.m., five days a week, with occasional overtime on the weekends when they needed it.

Running paper through a machine probably doesn't sound much better than working an assembly line, but the people I worked with spoke English and the hours were a little more humane, especially as I showed up early at 1st Athlete five days a week.

Having these two labor-intensive jobs during the summer before returning to college solidified one goal for me: I would never work at a job like these again.

In contrast, my experience at 1st Athlete couldn't have been better. I skated with players from the NHL, AHL, ECHL, European leagues, and NCAA Division I and III programs. I cherished every day I played that summer.

I was a very quiet guy in the locker room with all these great players. I would look at everyone's bags and be in awe at who I was sharing a bench with. Unless one of them asked me a question, I pretty much kept my mouth shut.

One day in late July after a scrimmage, Marty Sertich struck up a conversation with me. He had grown up in Roseville, Minnesota, and went on to win the Hobey Baker Award at Colorado College, enjoying a good AHL career before heading overseas. He had played in Switzerland the previous season and would be heading back there soon for training camp. He was the best player on the ice that summer, in my opinion. His vision and playmaking ability were the best I'd ever seen. Keep in mind that we were on the ice with NHL players too—players like Justin Braun, Jamie McBain, and others. I don't know how Marty never got a game in the NHL.

Marty asked me, "Where do you play?"

"University of Washington in Seattle," I said.

"Really?" he said, clearly shocked, as were most players in the locker room when they heard me say that. "Interesting. I don't know much about that program. Why are you playing there and not in the USHL or NCAA?"

So I shyly explained my story, as briefly as I could, with the whole locker room listening. None of the eight or so guys there knew anything about the ACHA, so I began fielding questions left and right. Those ten minutes of questioning made me feel like I actually belonged on the ice with these players. In my head, I already knew this just by skating with them. But having a great player like Marty showing interest in me meant they thought so, too. I could feel myself breaking out of my shell, opening up, and becoming comfortable with myself.

I am very appreciative of Marty's genuine curiosity that day, which led to a very different locker room experience with the rest of the guys. I no longer walked in, plopped down my bag, dressed in silence, did my thing on the ice, and left without saying a word. I now had the confidence to speak to these pro players because Marty made it clear I was just another one of the guys in the room, like him, out for a skate, trying to get better.

But one more important point came out of that conversation when, at the end, Marty said, "You know, you can be good enough to play in Europe if you keep working."

Now I had a new goal.

Chapter Five

Ryan Hockey

BACK AT UW FOR MY SOPHOMORE YEAR, I MOVED INTO AN APARTMENT with two of my teammates, Andrew Johnson and Mikey Remedios. We had become good friends as my freshman season went along, mainly because we were cooped up in the car traveling to and from every practice. After most parties I attended at the hockey house, rather than ending the night in my own bed, I typically slept on the couch at Mikey and Andrew's apartment.

The unfortunate part of living with two players older than me was how we picked bedrooms. They were juniors and pulled the seniority card, choosing the two decent-sized rooms in the complex. I got stuck with what could charitably be called a large closet for my bedroom. I had about three feet of walking space around my twin bed, desk, and the actual cubby-sized closet jammed full of clothes. Not an ideal setup, but it was my own bedroom. I felt lucky to be living out of the dorms with two guys I liked being around.

Going into the season, we hadn't heard of any new recruits joining the team. That caused some concern, considering we had lost several guys from the previous year's roster. Upon showing up to tryouts, we learned of two additions to our star-studded group. Kyle Umlauf, a junior civil engineering student who had decided not to play his sophomore year because he hated missing football games and needed to focus on academics, rejoined the club. The other new player was Alex Black, who came in as a freshman from Colorado and didn't join the team until the first week of the season, missing tryouts. The funny thing about club hockey is that players mysteriously come out of the woodwork. Some players on the team came to UW not knowing a club hockey team existed until they arrived on campus. Alex was one of those players.

The team welcomed two interns to the team: journalism student Tommy Fowler, who would be writing game summaries for the team website, and Abby Kozyra, a business student who would help with our marketing efforts. Relying on a bunch of disorganized college guys trying to attend classes, play hockey, manage the club details, and develop the program proved to be quite a challenge. We hoped adding two interns into the mix could lessen the load a bit, as well as bring in new ideas and energy. I thought maybe they could get my ideas of recruiting Ice Girls and live-streaming games off the ground.

We kicked off our season with a bang in Sin City, where we played against the University of Nevada, Las Vegas. Unfortunately for me, I was not yet twenty-one, so gambling and all the "adult" fun wasn't an option. Players over twenty-one made the most of their privilege. My parents made the trip to watch. It was my mom's first time seeing me play for UW in person, a great excuse to come to Vegas.

Instead of staying at one of the grand hotels, we were booked at a two-bit casino called the Fiesta Rancho, located a few miles off of the famous Vegas Strip but conveniently connected to SoBe Ice Arena, where our games were to be held. The games were scheduled at the prime time of midnight. We often played 10:00 p.m. home games in Seattle, but a midnight slot was a new level of ridiculousness. Our games followed a disco-themed open skate session, which is a nice way of saying to UNLV, "Nobody cares about you." Club hockey players were accustomed to this type of treatment when it came to fan support and arena availability. Many of our home games and practices my freshman year followed adult league learn-to-skate practices. It was just how it worked for some ACHA-level teams.

Like us, UNLV had made regionals last year, so we knew we were headed into a fierce battle. We split the series, which constituted a solid start—especially given our road woes the previous year. After the games, I walked aimlessly around the Strip with our other underage teammates and had breakfast at Denny's at 3:00 a.m. A few hours later on Sunday morning, those over twenty-one showed up to the airport minibus, drunk and slurring their words as they sloppily chatted up the driver on the way to our 8:00 a.m. flight back to Seattle.

I followed up our drunk upperclassmen's performance with a highlight of my own on our next road trip to Idaho, where we split the series against Boise State University. We all headed to dinner at the classy Applebee's across the street from our hotel. As we finished up our meals, we asked for our individual checks. My bill came to $12.71.

I was so rattled by getting chirped all meal by my teammates for my lack of attempted game with our lovely waitress that I absentmindedly walked out of the restaurant without paying. Dan Herda caught the mishap and paid my bill for me—but not without tacking on a generous $20 tip. I brought him the $32.71 to the next practice. I knew I was on pace to make myself the go-to standing joke of the team, if I hadn't achieved this honor already.

About a week later, my teammates gave me the nickname "Ryan Hockey" after Johnny Manziel famously was dubbed "Johnny Football." Teammates could never make enough Ryan Hockey jokes in the locker room, portraying me as some kind of magician on the ice who could do no wrong. We'd talk about NHL games, and if I turned to Alex Black in the locker room and said, "Yeah, that was a sick play," he'd smile wickedly and say, "He's no Ryan Hockey, though. Not as nice as Ryan Hockey woulda done it."

In more serious matters, the I-5 Cup that season played out before January. We split the first two games in Seattle and then got swept in Eugene. I don't have much to say about those games. They were painful. Disappointing. Soul-crushing. As always, all four games were hard fought. In the fourth game of the series, which we needed to win to force a shootout to decide the outcome of the series, I had a four-goal performance. But we came up one goal short, as Oregon won in overtime, 7–6, and took the I-5 Cup.

After the game that night, we started the long trek back to Seattle, on schedule to arrive home at around 3:00 a.m. Four packed cars drove through the darkness and rain in sorrow. I rode in Andrew Johnson's car, an aging Volvo. Sorrow turned to frustration as we suffered a flat tire just outside of Portland—at midnight, rain pouring down, in terrible conditions. But the worst had yet to come. Although we had the temporary good fortune to stop under an overpass to put on the spare, we could see it wouldn't last the more than 150 miles we still had to go. The tire was too skinny and didn't have much air. We hoped to make it to a gas station where we could pump it up, but we drove no more than 40 feet before stopping on the side of the road again. No sheltering overpass this time.

None of our teammates' cars were behind us on the road to stop and help, so we called AAA and ordered a tow truck. We figured they'd tow us to a tire shop, some auto mechanic would replace the tire, and then we could get back on our merry way, but this was not the case. No tire shops are open for business at 1:00 a.m. The tow truck took us and the car a few miles away to an empty Walmart parking lot, where we sleepily waited until 6:00 a.m. to have the tire replaced. I tried to rest in the car for a couple of hours, but the back seats didn't recline and the temperature outside hovered around freezing. It must not have been much warmer inside the car, as the windows frosted over, and I shivered all night. The Walmart employees quickly fixed the tire in the morning and got us back on the road.

After that disastrous trip, our woes continued. We were scheduled to play Western Washington University four times in a row, but we played only three of those games. I wish we hadn't played any of them. WWU delivered multiple concussions to our team, one of them to me in our second game of the series. I curled up the center of the ice in our defensive zone and got flattened even though I didn't have the puck. (Picture the Jack O'Callahan hit on Rob McClanahan in the movie *Miracle*, minus me getting up afterward and fighting. I was too dazed.) A nice, cheap shot.

Because of the concussion, I watched the third game, which we were hosting, from the stands. One of our players received a hard cross-check to the face at center ice during the middle of the second period, prompting a bit of a melee. As the scrum grew in steam and tempers flared on both sides, the WWU backup goalie grabbed a garbage can full of trash next to their bench and tossed it onto the ice, strewing litter everywhere.

You had to see it to believe it—an embarrassing display of hockey hooliganism and a disgrace to the game. Players spent the next five minutes attempting to clean it all off of the ice. The ref threw out the backup goalie and multiple players from each team. As a result of the antics in that game, we never played the final game of the series.

The ironic part of the whole series with WWU is their head coach was the father of Danny Dougan, our outstanding goalie from last season. You would think the guy would be somewhat respectful in the way he directed his players, since his son had played for UW, but that was not the case. He clearly had some unfinished business with UW. Once word got out after the game about these incidents, teams around the Northwest removed WWU from their schedule.

Our next road trip sent us to sunny San Diego to face San Diego State University for a much-needed escape from the dreary Northwest. In club hockey, however, a true escape doesn't exist. Upon arriving, we headed to our hotel, just minutes from the arena. As we checked in, we noticed quite a bit of construction being done on the hotel. We didn't think much of it—until we got to our rooms. When I opened the door, I was greeted by a familiar but unwelcome smell. Two steps into the room I found mold covering one of the walls.

But it got even better.

I wandered over to the sink and turned on the faucet. No water came out, not even a dribble. Then I tried to flush the toilet. Nothing. I walked out of my room and over to another teammate's room only to hear hysterical laughing. As I pushed open the door, I found a giggling Dan Herda.

"The toilet doesn't flush!"

This was a new low, even by club hockey standards.

The hotel looked like it had been abandoned. I couldn't believe the front desk clerk even let us check in. Why did none of us take a look around once we arrived? I doubted any other paying guests were actually staying there.

We knew the club hockey budget didn't allow us to stay at the Ritz-Carlton, but this fleabag was uninhabitable. No wonder it cost only $50 a night. Our intern, Abby, had successfully booked a handful of our hotels that season, including this one, to make our lives easier. When she heard what happened, she felt pretty bad.

We decided to find a new hotel, but not before this wreck of a hotel—where we stayed all of about twenty minutes—charged us for a one-night stay for each room, a budget-breaking $200.

The hotel we finally found sat right on Pacific Beach, which got us pretty fired up. To save some costs, we booked one room fewer than we'd planned, and Andrew Johnson and I slept in Coach Kell and Coach Stephenson's room, which had two beds. I slept with Kell, preferring the comfort of a mattress. Andrew slept on the floor because he didn't want to share a bed with Stephenson. I can tell you—the chainsaws were buzzin' all night in that room.

We played football in the sand and laid out on the beach the day of our game against SDSU, who were ranked in the region's top ten— probably not the best idea about how to prepare for the tough game ahead. We lost, 8–3.

After the game against SDSU, we won the next five of six games to head into the PAC-8 tournament with some momentum. One of those wins came against UCLA at home in front of a standing-room-only crowd—an unbelievable feat for us. Austin Seferian-Jenkins, a UW football tight end who eventually went onto the NFL, performed the ceremonial puck drop before the game. He gave a pregame pep talk, telling us to "'f*** people up." He took pictures with us and, best of all, showed up at our after-game party to hang out. We gave him some UW hockey team merchandise, which we had started selling that season, and he wore a signed UW jersey to the party, psyching me up.

The conference tournament was laid out differently than the simple four-team format from the previous year because the conference had been split up into North and South divisions. (The PAC-8 commissioner must have thought we were as cool as the PAC-12 Conference and wanted to follow their lead on conference alignment.) This year, six teams would reach the PAC-8 tournament. Each division had four teams: UW, WSU, Oregon, and Utah in the North; USC, UCLA, UC Berkeley (Cal), and Stanford in the South. The top three teams from each division made the tournament. Stanford and WSU were both awful, per usual, so the six teams attending the PAC-8 tournament, hosted by USC in Anaheim, were no surprise.

The tournament location made the trip even better. We were staying minutes away from Disneyland and would be able to take advantage of the warm winter weather Southern California had to offer in February. It definitely beat the gloomy, rainy winter in Seattle.

We came in as the fourth seed and faced off against fifth-seeded Cal in our first game. Because it was a night game, we had all day to explore the surrounding area. What better place to spend the day than at "The Happiest Place on Earth"? One problem: Coach Kell had told us before going down to Anaheim that we were not allowed to go to Disneyland. He worried we would tire ourselves out, and he wanted us to be on this trip for one reason—to win the PAC-8 Conference. A few teammates and I went anyway. No way was I going to miss out on a chance to go to Disneyland for the first time in my life. I had a blast. We got there right when the park opened at 8:00 a.m., so we went on plenty of rides without having to wait in long lines.

As a sophomore, I had clearly fallen into the ACHA mindset on road trips, treating them as vacations. During my freshman year, I saw all the fun my teammates had and decided I wanted to partake. Taking a more laid-back approach on trips didn't adversely affect my play; in fact, I think it helped me stay relaxed, as I stopped pressing so hard to perform. On the road, I just went out and played with confidence, and the rest took care of itself. Maturity played a part, and mentally I was much stronger than I had been the previous season. Any poor attitudes my teammates had didn't affect me. My mindset during games shifted, too. If I scored a goal or two in the first couple of periods, I was no longer satisfied with the job I had done on the ice. I stayed hungry for more, which helped me achieve my goals and pushed me to try and live up to "Ryan Hockey" standards.

After Disneyland, we were picked up by a van full of gear and team-mates and driven to Anaheim ICE. Naturally, Coach Kell found out about our excursion and was furious with us. Coaches Kell and Stephenson couldn't even talk to us before the game started. They walked into the locker room about ten minutes before we took the ice, scanned the room with obvious disgust, and walked right out—no pregame speech.

Those of us who went to Disneyland looked around at each other and couldn't hold back our laughter. We were ready to show them going to Disneyland wouldn't make an impact. That the coaches didn't bench those of us who went—at least for a little bit of the game—surprised me. Their will to win must have trumped the thought of teaching us a lesson, because I didn't miss a shift all game. We smoked Cal, winning 15–4. The five of us who went to Disneyland accounted for 11 out of the 15 goals that game, seemingly capitalizing on every scoring chance we had. We had one of those games in which we could not execute any better than we did, while the Cal goaltenders obviously had a rough day at the office. The best part about that game was proving to Coach Kell that going to Disneyland hadn't been an irresponsible choice.

Maybe we needed to hit up Disneyland more often before a game.

That win set up a return matchup with Oregon, where we lost another nail-biter—frustratingly similar to each I-5 Cup game we had played that season. Oregon went on to lose to Utah in the championship game, handing Utah their first ever PAC-8 Championship.

A nearby movie theater was the venue for the end-of-the-year banquet, where awards were presented on stage, giving them an added feel of importance. My teammates Andrew Johnson, Corey James, and Bryce Johnson made the PAC-8 third team, and I received the award I had set out to win, making the first team. I broke the school record for total points in a season and the PAC-8 season scoring record. My coaches praised my progression on the ice from my freshman season to now.

Once again, some of my favorite teammates would soon be graduating—Daniel Carson, Bryce Johnson, Kyle Rowe, Jordan Chernesky, and Daniel Herda, whose signature shot I would miss the most.

In one game, Herda kept hitting the goalie in the chest on golden scoring opportunities. Coach Stephenson advised him, "Herda, look at the goalie's chest when you shoot, then the puck might find its way into the corner of the net." This proved to be magical advice, as Herda scored a goal soon thereafter, snipping a top corner.

I would miss Jordan Chernesky's humor. He had the jokes rolling nonstop—sometimes taking them a bit too far, but undeniably a hilarious guy. Kyle Rowe, whom Jordan referred to as the "hippie" thanks to his somewhat unorthodox, organic-looking attire and affinity for saving the environment, would be missed for his bright personality. He often listened to James Brown and Jurassic 5. I once made the mistake of asking him how much a "batch" of weed costs, and, being the chill guy he was, he got quite a kick out of my naivete. (Evidently, you don't buy weed in batches, a rookie mistake he often roasted me for.) Bryce—the original "work hard, party hard" guy—operated on a different level of intensity than everyone else. He brought passion to whatever he did, whether destroying another team on the ice or partying into the wee hours. I would miss Carson for his excellent defense and all-around solid skills. He also seemed to effortlessly win the attention of attractive women on campus, an ability I greatly admired.

On a team level, we did not achieve any of the three main goals we had set: no I-5 Cup, no PAC-8 Championship, no regionals appearance. We seemed to lack the third-period intensity and focus that we enjoyed the previous season at our home games. Coming off the most successful season in program history, some players felt they had already achieved all they wanted to at UW and didn't really have the extra drive to finish games like we did before. One could call it a championship hangover of a season.

On a personal level, I did accomplish what I wanted—and more. I finished second in the ACHA in total points, I made third team West Region All-American (again hoping I'd finish higher in the region based on my season performance), and best of all, I was selected to the PAC-8 All-Star Team that would compete in Philadelphia in April. Although I was pleased with what I had achieved personally that season, I couldn't help being disappointed at the team level. I was determined to make my points more meaningful to generate wins.

In late April, Corey James and I boarded a plane to Philadelphia for the ACHA All-Star Tournament. Representing the PAC-8 Conference, we were going to show that the West Coast could hang with East Coast and Midwest teams. Because the majority of our PAC-8 team hailed from the West, I was curious how we would fare. I had never really gotten a chance to meet and talk with any players from other PAC-8 schools, so I looked forward to the opportunity to do so.

I found the all-star experience that year to be enlightening, even rejuvenating for my hockey career. It showed me that other players on PAC-8 teams faced the same challenges I did: Dealing with the stigma of playing club hockey, always overlooked and underappreciated by the administration and student body, playing under challenging conditions and at bizarre game times, enduring poor travel arrangements and sketchy accommodations, always contending with a shortage of money, and more.

PAC-8 Commissioner Johnny Nguyen picked Corey and me up from the airport upon our arrival. What we didn't know was that players selected for the tournament from our archrival Oregon had a flight landing about the same time. Nguyen loaded them up—four of them to our two—into the van as well.

Awkward is the only way to describe the ensuing car ride. We all sat in silence, with the exception of the Oregon players singing parts of the music off their teammate's iPhone that was blaring out of the speakers.

On our first night there, we had a short practice to set up the lines and meet the rest of the team. Coaches handed out our jerseys and socks for the tournament—our first inkling that this would be a much different experience than UW club hockey. Each uniform had stitched logos, numbers, and team patches for our respective universities. They were professionally made jerseys—completely unlike any club hockey gear I'd ever worn.

Afterward, Corey and I went out for Philly cheesesteaks with a couple of the guys from USC. My dad flew out to watch the games, so he hung out with us and partook in our sightseeing.

As the weekend went on, the players on our team got more comfortable around one another. Corey and I were able to put our rivalry with the Oregon players behind us and ended up getting along pretty well. I could sense the mutual respect among our teammates and was relieved to find that no player had any issues with anyone. I found the locker room vibe to be so different from how it was back at UW. All of the players shared an intense commitment to playing great hockey, brought a positive attitude to the locker room, and enjoyed their time out on the ice. Corey and I loved the environment, thriving on that feeling of wanting to be the best.

I had taken that attitude for granted when playing in Minnesota and missed feeling that positive power at UW.

The most memorable moment of the weekend for me came early Saturday morning during the first intermission of our second game. After a sluggish first period against a team we should have handled easily, we trailed by a goal. Mark Francis, the UCLA head coach and our PAC-8 team head coach, didn't waste any time ripping into us for our poor performance. In the final minutes of the period, I had missed a wide-open net off a one-timer on the power play after receiving a great pass across the slot from Corey. Francis called me out during his outburst: "Minkoff, you're the best player in the conference, one of the best in the league. You should be the best f***ing player on the ice!"

I didn't respond to that comment and just let him continue on his rant. He didn't say anything I didn't already know in my head, but I hadn't expected him to call me out in front of all of my teammates. Unfortunately, Francis's justified tirade didn't produce the needed results, as we lost the game and I finished with no points. In the end, we lost three out of the four games played and showed that we were not a top ACHA conference—at least not this weekend. Our only win came against the Atlantic Coast Conference in our final game.

Returning from Philadelphia with a determined attitude, I prepared to get all that I wanted out of the UW hockey program. I officially became the president in May, when the club's bank account transferred to my name. The balance read zero dollars and zero cents.

Like all successful presidents, I had to start by winning over my constituents—the fans. Publicizing the personal appearances and community activities we did to get the public behind us was at the top of my agenda. I made my first order of business as president to market merchandise. Dee Klem, who lived in Kent, Washington, had ordered a game-worn jersey for her son's birthday, coming up in just a couple of days. The cost of two-day shipping versus driving from Seattle to Kent and back was a wash. I borrowed Andrew Johnson's car and drove the forty minutes to her house for a personal hand-delivery. Upon arrival, I signed the jersey and presented it to her son on the spot. This young hockey player accepted the gift with a surprised and delighted smile, making my effort worthwhile. I spent the next half hour chatting with the Klem family, who let me know I had made their son feel special. This reminded me of times when I was little, attending University of Minnesota hockey games and meeting some of the players and being in awe.

Fans of UW hockey who weren't UW students really had no opportunity to interact with us as players. Playing our home games at 10:00 p.m. didn't help promote our cause; that UW even had a team wasn't common knowledge among the handful of general hockey fans in the area. I wanted to improve the interaction and awareness outside of the college-aged fans. Delivering a jersey in person proved to be an effective way of introducing our team and showing that we genuinely appreciated our fans.

The next change we made was to get new jerseys, finally addressing my very first complaint about the team. Our current jerseys were ugly, perpetually sweat-stained, and too heavy. With the help of my father— not only through his connections but because he covered the costs—we contracted Gemini Athletic to produce our team's new home and road jerseys. Chris Bonvino, the man who runs Gemini and who had helped get me into BSM, again worked with my dad on our new jerseys.

Next, I looked at our schedule and our opponents. The presidents in years past did not work on this task, leaving it for Coach Kell to complete. Why they didn't participate, I never understood, but I'm guessing it was most likely due to schoolwork and other priorities. I wanted to set up a schedule that didn't conflict with UW football games—many of which we missed—plus factor in a few fun road trips. I gave Coach Kell all the dates we needed to be playing at home if my plan to attend home football games that season was to work. Teammates expressed support for my stepping up to help design the schedule. Most players on the team found it frustrating that they could not attend every home football game. Trying to be a "man of the people," I negotiated with Coach Kell. I made the point that on the rare occasion that we were able to go to a game, we tailgated and sat together in the stands, which made for good team bonding. In the end, our schedule conflicted with only one home football game.

After that was taken care of, finding players to replace our seniors came next. Since we were a club team, students interested in playing college

Born to be a hockey player.

Where it all began with
the Hanover Hornets.

Ready to take on any challenger in mini sticks.

Buffalo Bison: It's not worth winning if you can't win big.

Minnesota Lightning: David Backes with the dark flow (top row middle), Joey Martin (right of him), Tony Cameranesi (bottom right).

Iconic Golden Gopher family picture.

My sister and I at the University of North Dakota hockey camp.

Minnesota SuperSeries: Jonny Brodzinski (top right next to the coaches), Christian Horn (left of Jonny), Travis Boyd (middle row directly below Christian), and me (top left next to the coaches).

Minnesota Pride: CAN/AM tournament in Lake Placid, New York.

Team Midwest: Craig Norwich taught me how to take a serious picture.

Tri City: We were Titans. The only season I ever used a Reebok hockey stick.

The real Hockeytown, USA: Warroad, Minnesota, with Wyatt Smith.

Armstrong Falcons: "A" stood for the sixty assists I registered that year.

Benilde-St. Margaret's: Rare shot of me on the ice.

Minnesota Wildcats: Where my career took off, playing against my buddy Jeff Spellmire.

UW hockey: Freshman year PAC-8 champs. PHOTO COURTESY OF CHRIS MAST

UW hockey: Greatest UW line ever assembled (From left to right: me, Corey James, and Alex Black).

UW hockey: We wouldn't miss out on the happiest place on earth.

Everett Silvertips training camp. PHOTO COURTESY OF CHRIS MAST

Virkiä: Arturs Ozols and I posing for the local newspaper. PHOTO: LEENA HJELT/*LAPUAN SANOMAT* (LOCAL NEWSPAPER)

Virkiä: Attempting to teach the young Finns about the United States.

Virkiä: After a big playoff win with Olli Mäenpää.

hockey had to be accepted based on their application, whereas Division I sports can pull strings in recruitment when a player does not have the average GPA or test scores—although some teammates joked that must have been how I got into UW. All I could do was try to find hockey players who already attended or would be attending UW in the fall. I worked with Coach Kell, who had a list of about twenty possible players, reaching out to those people to ask if they would be interested in playing. We received commitments from five players during the spring and summer months—not bad since we were losing five from the previous season.

As I wrapped up my sophomore year in June, I decided to stay in Seattle instead of going home to Minnesota for the summer. Andrew Mickus, an executive at Medbridge Education, a small start-up focusing on online physical therapy education, offered me a paid internship as a full-time business analyst for the summer. I agreed and looked forward to gaining valuable real-world business experience. After all, having an internship on my résumé would help with my backup plan if my "ACHA to the Show" master plan didn't work out.

I would be missing out on training at 1st Athlete during the summer, but I replaced this by playing in local men's leagues—a bit of a step down in training, to say the least. I joined two teams, one that played every Thursday night and one that played every Friday night, and worked out at the UW gym on campus a few days a week. I hoped I could keep my good form going into the next season.

The men's league teams I joined turned out to be of pretty good caliber, filled with a mixture of former and current junior, Division I, Division III, and pro players. Branden Vandermoon—or "Mooner" as we called him—one of my teammates at UW, helped me onto those teams, as he was already a member. Not only was it great to play with him, but we carpooled to the games, which built up our friendship.

One other guy who played on both of my men's league teams would prove to be an important factor in my summer: Mitch Love. Assistant coach of the Everett Silvertips in the Western Hockey League at the time, Mitch had also played in the American Hockey League. He became a household name as a player for the Silvertips when the team first came into the WHL in 2003.

That summer, my dad received an e-mail from Garry Davidson, the general manager of the Silvertips. It read as follows:

Jim,

Is your son RYAN??
We have our main camp in Everett, Aug. 21–25.
I would like to call you tomorrow to discuss.
Time and number please??

Garry Davidson
GM
Everett Silvertips

Pleasantly surprised by the e-mail, my dad decided to call him. I would have lost my mind if he hadn't. They had a brief chat about my attending the camp in August, and then Davidson said that he would be in contact with me over the summer.

I had always hoped for a shot at attending a WHL training camp while I was at UW. Now I might actually have that chance. I had just turned twenty years old in April, so technically I could play on the team, as the cutoff age was twenty-one. The team took only a couple of aged-out players—players like me who would age out of the league on our next birthday—every year, so my chances of making the team would be very slim. And I wouldn't play for the Silvertips even if I were to make the team; under NCAA rules, which the ACHA follows, a player who plays for a Major Junior hockey team becomes ineligible to play for a NCAA hockey team. I didn't want to lose my ACHA eligibility just yet.

My parents, who at one time had lived in Oregon, were fans of the Portland Winterhawks of the WHL and even became involved in some of the team's marketing and managing endeavors. From the stories I heard, they loved watching those games and helping out with the team, so I'd always had a positive impression of the WHL. I had been to a handful of Silvertips games while at UW, and they were fun to watch.

Since I played with Mitch on my men's league teams, I had the chance to get to know him a bit and learn about the possibility of trying out for the Silvertips. As the summer wore on, however, Davidson never contacted me. After some internal debate, I eventually went to Mitch and told him Davidson had approached my dad about my attending the Silvertips training camp.

"Let me talk to a couple people," he said, "and see what I can find out."

When he got back to me, he explained that because of my age, the coaches thought it would be silly to bring me into camp. Another point I had to consider: Each year the UW hockey team runs concessions at the Boeing Classic Golf Tournament—the same week as the Silvertips training camp in August. It would have been tough to attend the training camp anyway, because I'd have to be working shifts at the Boeing Classic each day.

To say I was crushed at not being able to go to camp would be an understatement. What a grand opportunity and experience—to play with NHL draft picks and some of the possible future stars in the WHL. But I had made a commitment to the UW team—my team—that I couldn't break.

And then, the day before the Silvertips training camp started, I got a phone call from Mitch: "Listen, we had a spot open up, and we'd like to bring you into training camp all week. Can you make it out to tonight's returning-player-only skate?"

An internal explosion lit me up inside. Still, as I remember it, I responded with professional calm: "Sure. Just let me know when to show up, and I'll be there."

When Mitch sent over the details, I decided somehow to make this all work. I had to figure out how I could put in my time at the Boeing Classic and still attend camp. The Boeing Classic required at least ten players to be working shifts at any given time to work three concession stands. As it stood, I had scrambled to get the minimum ten players to fill all of the slots. I knew a few players—probably more than a few—were not motivated to want to help out—so incredibly frustrating.

Despite my worry about players not showing up to the Boeing Classic, I managed to move around my Boeing Classic shifts to make both the Silvertips practice and the training camp. Andrew Johnson graciously let me borrow his car to get to the practice and training camp. I just had to pay for gas, and I was more than willing.

Practice with the Silvertips felt like being back at 1st Athlete. Players assumed I must be joining the team just by virtue of showing up. All the guys were welcoming, easygoing, talkative. I sat across from the likes of eventual NHLers Mirco Müller, Noah Juulsen, and a young Carter Hart. I put on my Silvertips practice jersey before hitting the ice like I was making my NHL debut, with care and precision, making sure I looked good.

Stepping onto the home ice of the Silvertips at Xfinity Arena (now called Angel of the Winds Arena) elevated my hockey experience to a whole new level. Instead of just a handful of the Silvertips coaching and scouting staff sitting in the stands, I imagined the arena filled with cheering fans. Team captains Matt Pufahl, Josh Winquist, and Kohl Bauml ran the team through a few passing drills and then we scrimmaged for the remainder of the time. I scored two goals during the scrimmage and thought I made a pretty good impression on the guys in the stands. I knew I could play with this team.

As the week went on, I managed to successfully juggle time at the Boeing Classic while attending the training camp, thanks to my creative scheduling. Luckily, our Boeing Classic concessions ran smoothly, with just enough players showing up to fill their scheduled time slots each day.

I performed pretty well all camp, skating with my fifteen- to twenty-year-old teammates. As an older player, I felt I should do well on the ice, even be a leader. Some of my teammates reminded me of myself when I was sixteen, with their minds focused on reaching their goals. Unlike me, the seventy-nine other players at the training camp were there to latch on with the Silvertips in some way—either by gaining a roster spot or at least getting on the radar of the coaching staff, hopefully to be brought up in a year or two. For me, the excellent competition and professional environment elevated my game.

Most of the players at the camp came from Canada—no surprise, as WHL rosters are filled with Canadians. I was the only player from Minnesota at the camp and the only college hockey player. During that week at camp, several people asked me why I played at UW instead of taking a different route—respectable hockey players and coaches questioning why, with my ability, I had chosen to play at the ACHA level. I took it as another sign of good things to come in my hockey career.

On championship Sunday, the last day of the Boeing Classic, I had one last early morning game. My training camp team had won all three of our games that week and was playing in the championship game. I had made sure the concession stands would be manned that morning so I could play.

I sat at Xfinity Arena putting on my gear when I received a call from the Boeing Classic staff giving me the worst possible news: We didn't have enough players to run the concessions. The UW hockey players scheduled to work that morning hadn't shown up. If we couldn't run a concession stand at the event, then our team would lose the projected two grand we'd receive for working the entire week.

As president, I shouldered the responsibility for fulfilling our team's commitment. Knowing we needed just two people, I went to work calling and texting several players. At 8:30 a.m. on a Sunday morning, I knew they were probably lying in their beds hungover, not in any shape to step up and help out.

No one responded. I was screwed.

So ten minutes before going on the ice for my game, I walked out of the locker room and found Mitch Love.

"Hey, Mitch, you got a minute?" I asked.

"Yeah bud, what's up?"

"I can't play in this game today," I said. "I have to go work the Boeing Classic because my teammates didn't show up to the shifts they were signed up for, and I'm responsible for the team. I'm really sorry, but I want to say thank you for this opportunity. It's been awesome and hopefully we can come out with the win today."

"No worries, Mink," he said. "We'll figure out the lines. We thought you looked good out here this week. Thanks for coming."

That conversation meant a lot moving forward. As my teammates headed out for warm-up, I quickly undressed and bolted to the car.

From that day forward, anytime anyone ever questioned my dedication to the UW hockey team, I could point to that sacrifice I made—the biggest disappointment up to that point in my life, it seemed. Even though I would not go on to play for the Silvertips, playing in that game meant everything to me. Hockey players work tirelessly from the time they can first hold a hockey stick just to reach such a point in their careers—to be invited to a top-echelon camp like this. I had achieved that goal but couldn't finish it out.

That my squad ended up winning lessened some of the pain. At least I hadn't let them down. But I would have relished the thrill of playing in and winning the camp's championship—not to mention getting my picture in the paper the next day with the rest of my teammates.

When I arrived at the Boeing Classic that Sunday morning, we were still short one person, but the Boeing Classic let us get away with having only three guys in each stand. A couple of hours later, another player showed up—four hours late—filling the shift I was scheduled to take after my hockey game. I could barely contain my fury. In the end, we covered enough of the shifts to get the promised $2,000 for our participation.

Following that weekend, Andrew, Mikey, and I planned to move into a six-bedroom apartment a couple of blocks from our previous place. We would be right near the heart of Greek Row, with a few fraternities and sororities surrounding our complex. I hoped the proximity to all these houses nearby would up my chances of meeting more women and finding someone I liked who liked me back. Mooner would be joining us in the apartment. Since we were just four people in a six-bedroom apartment, we knew the complex would assign two random roommates. We gambled and hoped for the best.

Unfortunately, right from the beginning we knew we were in trouble.

On move-in day we found our two roommates already ensconced in their rooms—so much for deciding fairly who got which room. One, a forty-something-year-old, who claimed to be a student at UW. I had my doubts, but we took his word for it. The other was a Chinese international student who pitched a tent—like you would take camping—to sleep in on the floor instead of a bed. Strange to say the least, but we kept an open mind and hoped all would work out.

Our main purpose for wanting a larger apartment was to be able to have people over, either to just hang out or to party after games. This idea wasn't looking too hot. Our older roommate posted signs all over the apartment designating his personal drawers in the kitchen, clarifying how clean the apartment needed to be, stipulating the complex's quiet hours (which we knew but figured no one followed), and outlining other "house rules." We just hoped when it came time to party, either he'd be gone or we'd just have to tell him to go to a movie.

That first week brought a sobering dose of reality topped off by a truly alarming event: Someone broke into our apartment during the night. Mikey's laptop and phone were stolen, as well as—weirdly—some food out of the fridge. Since our unit was located on the first floor and had a deck, anyone could easily climb up onto our patio from the sidewalk. Our screen door had—accidentally or not—been left unlocked, so the burglar came and went through that door. And it happened while we were sleeping, which made it all the more creepy. What a terrible and uncomfortable way to start our new living arrangements. A police report was filed, but nothing ever came of it.

The guy who lived in a tent moved out toward the end of September, replaced by a man in his late twenties. The first week in, he stole my food out of the fridge. A woman moved in with him, which was definitely not allowed under the lease agreement. We would have considered leaving and finding somewhere new, but breaking the lease we signed would have penalized each of us a couple of thousand dollars.

While struggling to make the best of the unfortunate living situation, I looked forward to beginning my junior hockey season. Outside of the team goals, I had my sights set on being the best player in the ACHA. Every year an ACHA Select Team traveled to Europe to play teams during the Christmas holidays, and I was aiming to receive an invitation. I hoped my sophomore season stats—finishing second in the league in points and making the Pac-8 All-Star team—would be enough to be offered this opportunity. I wanted to lead the ACHA in scoring, figuring I would likely need to break the 100-point mark.

Going into the season I felt optimistic and strong, like nothing could hold me back from ratcheting my play up a notch. I had set my personal goals and had the discipline to achieve them. My finishing ability, though good, could be improved, and I aimed to make this happen.

The week before our first games against the University of Idaho, I eagerly awaited my invitation to the ACHA Select Team. Instead, I received an e-mail saying they had decided to pass on me and thanked me for my interest. Not only did I feel I deserved to be on that team, but the opportunity would have provided me with invaluable exposure to professional hockey teams overseas.

Now I had a new goal: to show the coaches who picked the Select Team that they made a big mistake.

CHAPTER SIX

Rollercoaster Ride

EIGHT NEW PLAYERS JOINED THE TEAM: FOUR FROM OUT OF STATE (James Feldman, Christian Walsh, Quinlan Lonergan, and Bradyn Kawcak) and four from Washington (Keenan Smith, Terran Jendro, Troy Gasser, and J. D. White). I found the number of new players to be encouraging, as it was more than anticipated. As an upperclassman, I could see the team really beginning to turn over. On one hand, seeing my old teammates move on made me sad; on the other hand, I knew such changes were positive. Maybe these eager new faces would help create an even more positive environment.

Thankfully our best intern, Abby, reupped for another season and miraculously formed a whole crew of interns, an infusion of manpower that supported the team immensely. These interns helped not only in expanding our marketing efforts but also in selling merchandise, running the penalty box, operating the scoreboard, and managing other parts of game-day operations. Along with Susan White, mother of freshman forward J. D. White, Abby set up a concession stand at home games. This would be a profitable new addition to the UW hockey game experience, as BYOF (bring your own food) along with BYOB had previously been the only option. Susan White also provided the team with a fundraising opportunity at the retirement community where she worked; players could put in a few hours to move furniture within the complex in exchange for around $400 collectively. And finally—we would have Ice Girls. Abby took my idea and acted on it. I guess she didn't scare off the prospects like I did.

I'll admit to being curious how the Ice Girls would work out during our games. Typically, Ice Girls go out onto the ice during stoppages in a game, sometimes to shovel off the ground-up ice or figure skate to entertain the crowd. Abby told me only a couple of our Ice Girls could skate, so I really had no idea what they planned to do at our games. Nevertheless, the idea that we'd have at least a few more women in the stands at our games brought additional excitement to the coming season.

After the first two home games of the season, where we blew out the University of Idaho, we headed to the potato state to face Boise State. This trip would be the start to a season that would be memorable—for the good and the bad and even the bizarre.

Changes that had begun with new players continued with the coaches. Coach Kell was involved in a serious car crash before the season began, leading to his absence for much of the season and ultimately his retirement from coaching that year. Then Coach Stephenson moved into a more administrative role in the program. The previous season, we had added Assistant Coach Matt Cleeton, who had played club hockey as a goaltender at the University of Illinois Urbana-Champaign. And in the fall, another coach came on board: Zach Richardson, who had played defense for the Colorado State University club hockey program. Richardson, who became a father shortly after joining us, ended up being available only intermittently, which left Cleeton doing just about all of the coaching by himself. Coaching our team brought in no income—it was an entirely volunteer effort. Thankfully, one man was willing to give up his time for us that season.

Days before heading to Boise, we organized carpools among ourselves for the roughly eight-hour drive from Seattle. Fourteen of us would be heading on the road trip in four cars, one driven by Cleeton. Two players who had the cash booked round-trip flights to avoid the long ride. If only we had all been able to do that, so much heartache and drama could have been avoided. We didn't even think about the idea of taking a bus together because the cost seemed too high for our college budget.

Three cars made it to Boise in one piece; one car did not. With his three passengers asleep, the driver realized he had taken the wrong route, checked his phone for directions, got too close to the car in front of him, and slammed on the brakes, which led to the car rolling off the road and landing upside down—totaled. To the amazement of everyone, all four players in the car came out unscathed.

Coach Kell notified the UW Club Sports Department of the accident, so I didn't have to follow up. As a result of the accident, not only did those four players have no way to get to Boise, but one of the players who was flying had sent his hockey bag strapped to the top of that car. He lost his gear to save a few bucks on baggage fees, although in retrospect, having his bag on top of the car may have helped save those players' lives. So, all five players spent the weekend back in Seattle, putting the total team down to eight skaters for the weekend and just our backup goalie, as Jacob Gilmore didn't make the trip to Boise due to a family conflict.

We lost the first game, 15–1, and forfeited the second after two periods. We had only five players and a goalie available going into the third period of the second game due to injuries suffered in the first game, so we called it quits.

The journey back to Seattle from Boise brought more adventure. Christian Walsh's thirty-year-old car—in which I was riding with Mikey and Mooner—died two hours from Seattle near the college town of Ellensburg, Washington. Christian had family about an hour away, near the alpine-themed town of Leavenworth. He arranged to be picked up by his relatives, choosing to get someone to fix his car the next day. He offered for us to tag along, but since he planned to spend the night, that would mean we'd miss our classes on Monday.

The three of us decided to see if we could hitch a ride home. It took about twenty minutes of waving at cars from the side of the highway before someone pulled over. The man who stopped for us happened to be a good guy—a Native American and a Vietnam War veteran on his way to his grandson's football game in Seattle. We knew that hitchhiking could be potentially dangerous, but we felt desperate and without any other options. There were no taxis in these parts and no Uber yet. Luckily, the right person stopped for us, and we all got back home safely.

Obviously, this was a horrible start to our road season. We got some pretty harsh news later about the car crash on the way to Boise: The four players in the car had been smoking marijuana, including the driver.

Cleeton punished them by having them sit out a couple of our next games, a road trip to Spokane to face Gonzaga University and Washington State University. We won all three games, one versus GU and two versus WSU. I had an 11-point game in one of the WSU games, the highlight for me on the trip. The other highlight was that even though we carpooled once again, there were no accidents or breakdowns.

But we didn't come out of that trip unscathed. One of the players who sat out because of Coach Cleeton's punishment threw away an empty beer can in the Eastern Washington University arena where we had faced WSU—an unbelievably stupid move, as several signs in the locker room explicitly warned players not to discard alcohol containers on school property. If caught, the offender would be reported.

EWU reported that incident directly to the UW Club Sports Department, which then did some digging and uncovered the damning details of the car crash.

The Club Sports Department can shut down a program for incidents such as these. As president of the club, I had to step up and take responsibility, so a long meeting ensued with the department about the two incidents. The main question they put to me was this: Why hadn't I reported the incidents?

I was a little blindsided going into the meeting. I didn't know about the beer can incident until the department told me. I did know about the car crash and the weed, though, but didn't report it. Coach Kell said he would take care of the situation and that I didn't need to do anything further. The department didn't buy that. They pointed out that I was the one in charge of the program, not the coaches. I should have reported the incidents along with Kell, but I didn't. Lesson learned—and learned the hard way.

I accepted responsibility. I had to make a lot of apologies and ultimately shouldered the blame. The department decided to put our team on two years' probation, which meant we would not receive any funding to our program for that entire time—a loss of $3,600 each season. For a program that constantly struggled to fund itself, this represented a huge financial blow. Somehow, no players were dismissed from the team, but it was a rough situation whose effects lingered on for the rest of the season.

On top of this, our team did not have players of the caliber it had when I first joined as a freshman. That's how teams go. I came in at the all-time high, and now we were transitioning into a rebuilding phase. We no longer were unbeatable at home and we exhibited a lackluster attitude on the road. Almost all of our scoring came from the line I played on with Corey James and Alex Black. The team just lacked depth.

Mentally, I never felt completely satisfied during any game that season. If I had a hat trick in the first period, I felt I needed to score more. I knew if I let up we could lose, and if I wanted to reach my individual goals that year, I had to keep the pedal to the metal.

Then we played a midnight game in Oakland against the University of California, Berkeley. We had a horrid first period; starting off slowly had become a habit of this team. At the beginning of the second period, my line started clicking. Collectively, we potted four goals on four consecutive shifts. That's when I started believing our line could score a goal—or at least generate a scoring chance—every shift. My line mates bought into that mindset, too. It was a completely unrealistic ideal, to be sure, but I wanted to strive for that perfection the rest of the season. This shift in mentality brought a heightened level of intensity, energy, and quality of play to our line's game. That pretty much put me on the path to lead the nation in scoring, which I did.

Our next game—also against Cal—was the following night, with a starting time around 1:00 a.m. Every time some absurdity in the ACHA surfaced, something more unbelievable eventually came along to top it. I thought playing at midnight after an open skate session at UNLV was pathetic, but even worse was a 1:00 a.m. game that followed . . . nothing on the ice before it. Somewhere, the hockey gods must have been laughing.

To make this game even worse, Cal had no backup goalie, and of course their starting goalie got injured in the second period. They were forced to put a skater in goal. Their best player, Bryce Morisako—whom I'd played on a line with at the all-star tournament—suited up. He held his own for the most part, but I did get a hat trick in one shift during the third period. I really did show no mercy.

As this season continued, I always had our team goals in sight, and I wanted to win the I-5 Cup to help resurrect the season.

That year the games would be played on back-to-back weekends. We hosted the first two games of the series, splitting them as we had the previous year. And again, just like the year before, we lost the first game of the series in Eugene, setting up a must-win situation in the fourth game of the series. We held onto the victory in the fourth game, winning 3–2 even though Oregon had seven men on the ice in the final minute and the refs somehow missed it. This meant victory in the I-5 Cup came down to a five-man shootout.

Our goalie, Jacob Gilmore, had proven to be excellent in shootout situations—at least in practice—so I figured we would only need one or two goals to get the shootout victory.

My line mates were the first two to go. Both missed their attempts trying to deke out the goalie, but Oregon's guys missed too. I went third. I took a deep breath and thought about what my dad had told me so many times: If you shoot on a breakaway or shootout, make sure you are far enough out to not cut down your own angle, which gives the goalie a better chance to save the shot.

I took the puck from the center ice faceoff circle and skated in with a little speed. The goalie stayed relatively deep in his crease from the out-set, so I knew I likely would be shooting. Nearing the slot, I brought the puck in toward my body, which caused the goalie to slightly move off his angle. When I released the shot, his misalignment allowed the puck to go sailing cleanly into the back of the net's lower right corner.

What a relief. I pointed to the heavens and whispered a silent, "Thank God! Thank you, Dad!"

All of the shootout attempts and breakaways I had missed in my youth paid off right then and there. I wouldn't have had my father's tip ingrained in my head if I hadn't blown so many chances growing up. The next two Oregon shooters were robbed by Gilmore, so we had the chance to seal the deal with one more goal. Jason Bartlett took our next attempt and, as I had, shot the puck from the top of the slot and past the goalie. That victory meant more to our team than any other during that tumultuous season.

For the first time since I began playing at UW, we held a senior night event on the ice prior to the last home game, which would be played against Boise. Along with Abby and the coaches, I wanted to recognize our seniors, something I was surprised had never been done in previous seasons. Recognition is hard to come by in club hockey, so it seemed fitting to honor seniors for their contributions. I regretted that I hadn't thought of staging such an event for the seniors I played with during my freshman and sophomore years.

I also wanted to honor Abby for her help over the past two seasons. Outside of the team, nobody knew how much she did for us. Although she wasn't a player, she cared more about the team's well-being than most of the guys on the team. All the seniors and Abby came out onto the ice, along with family members or close friends, and the announcer said a few words about each one. It felt good to honor our departing players and Abby, and I looked forward to sharing the event next year with my parents.

We came into the PAC-8 Conference Tournament, hosted by Utah in Salt Lake City, as the number-four seed. The league and the tournament followed the same format as the previous season, with six teams qualifying. Unfortunately for us, we had to face Utah in the first round of the playoffs.

Because Utah consistently dominated us every season on the road, we went into this game with a defeatist attitude. We hoped Gilmore would stand on his head in net, giving us a chance to sneak a goal or two by the Utah goalie for a win.

As we tried to psych ourselves up for the game, we waited . . . and waited . . . for the shuttle bus provided by the host school to take us to the arena. Somehow, we were conveniently "forgotten," so our team had to walk thirty minutes to the venue, arriving late. Not a good start. It probably didn't make much difference, as we got manhandled, losing 10–1.

For me, the coolest part about this game came from the Utah broadcasting crew, who streamed the game online. They had someone interview me—my one and only video interview while playing at UW, which was a real thrill. Again, it was difficult to get recognition or publicity at the club level. Even when you led the nation in points—as I did all season long—nobody outside the rink seemed to know. I knew if I was ever going to get any press, I would have to do something special.

We played USC to wrap up our year at the PAC-8 tournament in a meaningless game—one of the more fun ones played during the season and my last ever with my favorite line mate, Corey James. The chemistry we had was incredible, and it got better each year I played with him. I could often blindly throw the puck to where I thought he'd be on the ice, and he'd be right there to receive it. He would be greatly missed. We won a high-scoring affair, 5–4, and Corey and I each had goals.

At the PAC-8 banquet, four UW players—Andrew Johnson, Jacob Gilmore, Corey James, and I—made the first team, with one player from Utah. It was a sweet ending to an average season, and somewhat insulting to other teams in the league. The league would remember this at the end-of-season awards the following year, but I can say we all deserved the awards based on our stats and individual performances on the ice within the conference. Still, it clearly showed that, for team success, we needed more depth than just the four of us.

As a team, we didn't accomplish all of our goals. Winning the I-5 Cup was the highlight for sure. On the ice, we had a lot to improve upon going into the next season. But off the ice, we had great success.

Our home game attendance and sales increased for the third year in a row. The team had steadily generated more awareness and interest, which boosted our morale. Steve Hobs, a member of the Washington State Senate, brought his family to watch us play Washington State University. And although most couldn't skate, the Ice Girls did help with marketing the team and provided some added fan interaction during games, leading cheers and just providing additional interest to the games. They formed their own separate club, which seemed encouraging, and I looked forward to what they would do in the upcoming year.

Personally, I achieved the kind of year I set out to have. I led the nation in scoring, with 108 points in twenty-seven games, ahead of the second-place guy by nearly 30 points. I kept a positive mindset and never let anyone bring me down mentally. Without sounding arrogant, I hoped my stats confirmed that I was one of the strongest players in the league. That season will forever remain a special—and unforgettable—one for me.

The seniors who were leaving the team were my favorites. I'd had three years to get to know them, and they were my best friends at UW.

Just about every fun activity I did outside the ice rink was with them: football games, basketball games, a couple of classes, golfing, Mariners games, outdoor activities—I enjoyed all those good times with them.

After the season, we formally made Assistant Coach Cleeton—who had stepped up to essentially run the team the whole year—our head coach for next season. Coach Kell's ten-year tenure officially came to an end. Cleeton and I worked well together, and we enjoyed a mutual trust, to the point where he let me set up the entire game schedule for my senior season.

That summer, I planned to stay in Seattle again and play on the same two men's league teams. While I had enjoyed my internship the previous summer at Medbridge Education, this summer I had another paid internship as a business analyst at Alstom Grid, a power and energy company that was acquired by GE during my summer there. This opportunity provided me invaluable experience in the corporate environment. The company was located in Redmond, Washington, roughly twenty-five minutes from my apartment by car—which I didn't have. Instead, I had to take two buses to get there, a ninety-minute commute each way. Though it was brutal at first, I eventually found a productive way to use that time, either reading books or writing. In fact, I began writing this book on that daily commute.

Through Coach Kell, I received an invite to an ECHL tryout in late August with the Florida Everblades. While I was flattered, I knew I couldn't attend. I hadn't yet finished school, and I didn't want to allocate my limited funds to fly to Florida for a weekend that was likely just a moneymaker for that team. I thought, *Maybe next year if I have no other options*. Nonetheless, the invitation reassured to me that there was a path to playing professional hockey through the ACHA.

Once again, a bunch of my teammates and I ran concession stands at the Boeing Classic Golf Tournament. Even though the work could be boring at times—and hard on your feet—we looked forward to the tournament because we could watch golf and eat free food for a week. Granted, hamburgers, fries, and beer might not have been the healthiest way to eat, but free meals are appreciated by every poor college student. On the last day, after the tournament ended, those of us working took home around a combined $500 worth of food and drinks, leftover inventory from our concession stands. I now had snacks covered for at least the next couple months.

During this season, the team finally got on YouTube. I had been pushing for a YouTube channel because a search for "UW Husky Hockey" on YouTube produced as its first result a video that showed USC scoring a late goal against UW in the PAC-8 tournament. I was sick of not having any positive footage of our team, so an intern and I put together a brief highlight video and launched the UW Hockey YouTube channel.

Meanwhile, I was facing an internal dilemma. Over the course of the past three seasons, I felt I had probably suffered two or three concussions, but I didn't know for sure because I was never examined by a doctor during the games.

All the recent studies and widespread concerns about head injuries made me worried about continuing my career. The wise choice may have been to retire to men's league, where I wouldn't have to worry about dangerous, physical contact. But if I left the team, it would be a blow to the UW program. I thought of my options: run the team as president but not play; be president and suit up for select games where I might be needed, like the PAC-8 tournament and I-5 Cup; or just play smart, pick my spots, and avoid the corners—where injuries most often occur—and play out the season.

I wanted to play my senior year, but I had to ask myself if it was a smart thing to do. I decided I would go forward on a game-by-game basis. If I experienced anything close to a concussion—or actually did suffer one—I would quit and simply run the team.

I wasn't sure if this was a very smart decision, but it was one I could live with. Thankfully, I skated through the season without taking a major hit.

Going into my junior year, I really hoped to find a girlfriend—not just a fling, but someone I cared about and could develop a relationship with. I didn't know how I would pull this off, other than showing up to every social gathering I was invited to and hoping for the best.

One night after a home game where we had just been crushed by Utah, 10–1, I stopped by teammate Bradyn Kawcak's house just to have a beer or two before going to bed. When I arrived, I found the scene very low key—Bradyn, his three roommates, and a couple of girls just hanging out. They invited me in and we all decided to play a drinking game to get our spirits up. The game centered around categories. NFL teams was one category, so we went around in a circle and fired off team names. If you couldn't name one, you had to drink. Being a good Minnesota boy, I started with "Minnesota Vikings," but the girl across from me—we'll call her Ashley—ended up tongue-tied, so she had to take a drink.

"Why did you say the Vikings?" she asked me later.

"I'm from Minnesota."

"Oh! Me too!" she said, giving me a brilliant smile.

So we had something in common to start. As the night wore on, we seemed to get along well, laughing together and just enjoying each other's company. When I walked Ashley back to her apartment, she invited me up to her room.

It didn't take long for me to fall in love, not just because she was smart and attractive, but because we enjoyed so many of the same things: hiking, cooking, watching sports, exploring the outdoors, hanging out with friends. I had no idea how great it would be to have a partner in all aspects of my life. Having a real girlfriend for the first time—kind of late, as I was almost twenty-one—made every experience better. That is love, and for the first time in my life, I felt its grip.

I did everything I could to learn new things along with her and to join in with her in whatever activities she did, and she appreciated my efforts. She had a free spirit, which I found to be refreshing and fun. I had always been a by-the-book kind of guy, so I let her free-and-easy mindset rub off on me.

My teammates couldn't believe I finally had a girlfriend, but they supported me. As the relationship developed, though, I spent less and less time hanging around my roommates. I dedicated my free time to Ashley first and foremost, which hurt my relationships with my roommates. I didn't realize this at the time, because love is blind. I was in love and tried to act how I thought a good boyfriend should.

Unfortunately, this meant I was lacking balance in my life.

Heading into the summer months, Ashley and I took a few great trips, most notably to some of the many gorgeous islands in and near Washington state. We took a trip to Victoria, British Columbia—a beautiful English-like city on Vancouver Island—and one to Whidbey Island and Deception Pass, with the majestic Olympic Mountains in the distance. And we took a couple trips to Minnesota to see our families and hit the state fair. I loved them all and had such a great time, and I enjoyed meeting her family, who treated me very well.

And then, in early August, it all came to a screeching halt. I had no clue. I woke up to a phone call from her near 1:00 a.m. asking me to meet her at Denny Field—a huge green expanse where we often played sports. She showed up looking beautiful and then said the unexpected words: "Sorry, it's over."

"What?" I sputtered. "Why?"

And then she gave the most clichéd excuse ever. "It's not you; it's me."

As I stared at her in disbelief, she explained that she needed to figure out what she wanted in life. Devastated, I went home, just completely mind-blown and feeling numb.

A few days later, Ashley texted me, asking if we could get together. We met up and once again started hanging out. I wondered if she was rethinking her decision to break up. I hoped that somehow we would be able to mend our relationship.

For the next few weeks, we spent time together without officially being boyfriend/girlfriend, but I still treated her that way. However, I began to feel like she was using me as a prop until she found someone else.

When my summer internship ended, I planned to spend the evening with her to celebrate, although we had no concrete plans set. We both had moved to different houses during this time, and she was conveniently now three doors down. I moved to a new hockey house with five other returning teammates—a much better experience than the previous year's apartment with strange roommates and fewer opportunities to hang with friends. This house had a pretty sweet setup—a couple of TVs, gaming consoles, two kitchens, a washer and dryer, and plenty of seating and space for parties.

That night, as I sat on my front porch reading a book around 9:00 p.m. waiting for a text back from Ashley, I watched a guy walk up the steps of Ashley's house. He turned out to be her new boyfriend.

A couple days later, Ashley asked to meet me. She said she had found someone else and no longer wanted to see me. It hurt to hear this, as I still had feelings for her, but despite the loss, the experience helped to boost my confidence. I realized I was a good person, worthy of having someone care for me. And I learned a lot, most notably: Don't give up everything for a relationship. I guess a lot of us have to learn that lesson.

Forgiving myself for being lovestruck and asking my roommates to give me a break—which they did, as some of them had been through the same experience—became my pathway back to being whole. I ended up thankful I went through what I did, knowing it would help me mature. And I channeled the hurt and rejection into what I knew best—hockey.

Chapter Seven

Farewell Tour

My senior year would be my grand finale at UW. That year my parents also decided to uproot from Minnesota after nearly twenty-five years and move to Lake Stevens, Washington, a picturesque community about thirty miles north of Seattle. They had been planning for quite some time to move closer to my mom's family and get out of the cold, so they spent the summer months selling their house. I couldn't help feel this house had provided a unique place to spend my childhood. The property, nestled in between a small farm and pastures with a neighbor's horses, had a big barn and five acres of land to explore and enjoy all sorts of creative play. With my mom running a preschool and daycare in our basement, I'd wake up at 7:00 a.m. to yelling and laughing kids right below my bedroom, where I would eventually go downstairs to play with everyone. Participating in hide-and-seek on five acres against four-to-eight-year-olds is quite the task, as one game could seemingly last for hours. My sister and I also spent time shooting hoops, shooting pucks in the pole barn, and having bicycle and sled races. One of my other favorite memories of the house is playing baseball in the front yard with my father. He would stand at one end of the giant lawn, bat in hand, and hit baseballs to me. A couple hundred feet away, I'd catch the flies and field the grounders—or run after them.

The sale of my parents' home was a bittersweet moment for me— I was sad that I would never go back to my childhood home, but so happy to have my parents nearby. And selfishly, I was glad I would now have access to a vehicle on occasion. But the biggest bonus was that my parents would be able to come to all my home games that year, which brought a new level of excitement and anticipation to the season.

After my final hockey season, I would be handing off the torch of UW hockey to the president-elect, Troy Gasser. Troy lived with me in the new hockey house, so it was easy to keep him clued in to what I, the interns, the coaches, the UW Club Sports Department, and others were trying to accomplish with the program. I planned to make sure he was more prepared than any previous president when he assumed the role.

When I took the helm, all I got was a box of merchandise filled with assorted sweatshirts and T-shirts, the UW Ice Hockey checkbook, a debit card (tied to an account with zero funds), and the wise words, "Good luck." Why hadn't Herda given me all the relevant info he and other past presidents had collected about how to make our team successful? Past years' budgets, e-mails about scheduling games and fundraising efforts, contacts for sponsors, how to book (or avoid) hotels in various cities, and other information would have been helpful.

I wasn't given much guidance or direction, nor did I really ask for any, which was my own fault; in my defense, I didn't know what I needed. All our team presidents were just kids like me—young hockey players trying to figure out real-world problems between games and classes. It had always been a "fly by the seat of your pants" kind of operation. That's no knock; it's just how it had been done in the past.

Presidents handed off the torch to the next person, and the new president got to experience the job as trial by fire. I knew I could do better. I planned to set a new standard for passing on information, which would make running the team less stressful and chaotic.

I put together a folder containing all the info I had gathered in my two years as president. I knew Troy, a capable and smart engineering student who cared about the program, would have no problem using the this resource. I felt I was leaving the UW hockey program in good hands and well prepared.

I had high aspirations for myself going into the season. To have a shot at pro hockey afterward, I felt I needed to have a season worthy of possibly getting inducted into the ACHA Hall of Fame one day. There were just fourteen members in the Hall of Fame at the time, so this was a lofty goal. One member, Glenn Detulleo, amassed 318 points in 131 games at Iowa State before going pro in Norway. I had 284 points in 81 games going into my senior year, so I thought I could be in the discussion with another strong statistical season. I also wanted to prove that I could have a good year without Corey James, who had been my primary linemate the past three seasons. I hoped we'd gain some good incoming freshmen to try to replace him.

Tryouts got underway a few days before classes started. A handful of new additions to the team showed up, including one goalie, Thatcher Givens; two defensemen, Josh McGrew and Simon Machalek; and four forwards, Austin Hutchinson, Tyler Jennings, Cory Tung, and Joe Kinkopf. All of the new recruits were good guys, fun to be around, and great additions to the team.

Thatcher was a character and the leading gym rat on our team, always working out. After one year with the team, he would leave to attend the Naval Academy. Josh came to UW from Nicaragua, where his parents did missionary work, so he had a strong religious background. One of the nicest guys I've ever met, he and his Christian frat hosted barbeques every week; I came and ate a bunch of free food and met some exceptionally good people. Simon came from a high school in Boston, but he was originally from the Czech Republic, where his family still lives. We got along really well. Austin lasted only a quarter of the season due to a bad back. Tyler would end up being my line mate alongside Alex Black for the season. He was a nice but very quiet guy—not unlike me in my first year. I didn't get to know him all that well, but he worked well with Black and me on the ice. Cory was responsible for many of the pranks pulled throughout the season. He lived with a great bunch of roommates, so I hung around with them throughout the year. Joe was "the man"—an idol of sorts for me and others on the team, as he seemingly won over every woman he saw. The ultimate frat star, he sometimes put me on the guest list for his frat parties.

When I worked on scheduling games over the summer, I got confirmation from every school except Washington State. It took me four months to get our season schedule completed. Organizationally, the WSU team was a disaster. Nobody wanted to step up and run the team.

We finally arranged the four games we usually play against them a month before the season began, and our first games of the season were against WSU in Spokane.

Only Gilmore and I remained from the team that had gone to regionals during my freshman season. I knew this meant I had to carry the load more this season than ever before. Based on what we saw in practices, the newcomers didn't seem to be top-tier talent, so if we were going to win, this year's team would be forced to rely on a combined effort rather than the skill and talent of a few players. We couldn't get away with playing lazy defense or sleepwalking through periods against any team, even WSU. Every game promised to be more competitive than what I'd experienced in the previous three seasons. I was now the old man on a young, inexperienced team. It was up to me to show the players the way.

WSU's team had been built in a similar fashion to ours, with the exception of goaltending. Both teams relied on just one line to do the heavy lifting—meaning they accounted for most of the scoring—and the rest of the team just needed to hold their own. Thankfully, we had a much better goaltender than WSU, so we were able to sweep the opening road series to get off to a 2–0 start.

USC visited us for our first home games, and we knew they would be a tougher test than WSU. Unfortunately, we got swept at home. That had rarely happened in my entire career at UW, so my teammates and I were more than surprised and displeased with our performance.

We then went down to Eugene to face off against the Ducks for the first half of the I-5 Cup. Unlike the late starts of UW's home games, Oregon scheduled the Friday night game for 7:00 p.m. It usually takes around five hours to travel from Seattle to Eugene, so we left a little after noon, carpooling in rented vans for the first time on a road trip. I made sure we traveled the smart and safe way that year. Thanks to absolutely horrendous traffic, we didn't even make it to the arena until 8:10 p.m. We had to call the school and ask them to push the start time back. They were nice enough not to insist we forfeit.

When we got onto the ice for warm-ups at around 8:30, I noticed they had a pretty big student section at the game. A couple of the fans in the front row wearing Mighty Ducks jerseys began chirping at me.

I couldn't help but laugh at some of the things they said. During the national anthem they even yelled at me, "Put your hand on your f***ing heart, Captain!" Those fans left after the first period ended, which was too bad, because that kind of razzing fired me up. But they probably needed to find a bar to keep their buzz going.

As for the games against Oregon, we got manhandled, 9–5 and 7–2. As a team, we played with a lack of intensity, which was frustrating to me, as that was the kind of low-energy vibe I most wanted to change. For the most part, this lack of inspirational play carried through the season until January.

We knew we weren't going to make regionals but would likely make the PAC-8 tournament no matter what, so what difference did it make whether we won or lost during the season? I put that fundamentally poor thinking on myself. "Attitude reflects leadership, Captain," as Julius said in the movie *Remember the Titans*.

We finished out the first half of the season with a 6–9–1–1 record, with four of those wins coming from forfeits by Portland State and WSU. So, in my mind, I considered our record to be 2–9–1–1. Awful—and we had some notable losses during this stretch.

Our trip to Los Angeles, where we faced UCLA twice at the old LA Kings practice arena and Cal State Northridge once, was a fun trip off the ice, but not on it. On the way to the Northridge game, I followed Jacob Gilmore's van and nearly crashed multiple times trying to keep up with him as he weaved through traffic. He loved messing with me on road trips. He would pull off at an exit, drive into a parking lot, do a few circles, and then beeline back to the highway. It drove me nuts. I would follow him because I always assumed he knew where we were going, but he took advantage of my reliance on his directions.

Northridge had a solid team, and we knew we would have to fight hard. The funny part about this game was that we had only about two lines of players for the entirety of the game. A couple of players were flying in the next day and missing this game. Cleeton gave his pregame speech, and after he left the room, my teammates joked and proclaimed the game plan: "Unless your name is Minkoff, dump the puck in." We actually held our own for most of the game with the effective game plan in mind, and I had a couple of goals, but we let it slip away in the third period and lost, 8–4. Then UCLA swept us in two games with nearly identical scores—4–2 and 4–3. We held a one-goal lead going into the third period of each of these games. I had only a couple of points in both games, my worst two-game stretch since my freshman season. I played terribly, and I put that series sweep on myself. If I had played at my best, there's no way we would have lost those games.

Finishing the first half of the season against Utah at home, we knew we'd likely get smoked. Before the first game, the Utah head coach approached my father in the stands. My dad was apparently pointed out to him by a parent.

"Hey, Jim," he said, as though they were friends, "we're going to be coming after your son tonight. Our goal is to knock him out of the game since we already know we'll win." My dad looked back at him in amazement, shook his head, and walked away.

The game wouldn't be close even if they left me alone, so I found those comments ridiculous. My dad texted to tell me what the coach had said and told me to keep my head up.

I have never hated an organization more than I hated Utah, even our biggest rival, Oregon. I respected Oregon. I did not respect Utah because they took cheap shots and tried to take my head off.

Off of the opening faceoff, about ten seconds into the game, Utah's defenseman hit and flipped me into their bench, where other Utah players from the bench yanked me over. I then drew a penalty on Utah in the same shift a half a minute later. Talk about an insane first shift. Later in the period, the Utah coach's kid, a defenseman, took about a forty-foot run at trying to put me through the glass. I saw him coming but pretended I didn't know he was there. At the last minute, I stopped quickly and changed direction. He missed me, plowed himself into the boards, and knocked himself out of the game. They still destroyed us in both games, 8–1 and 9–1. I scored one of the goals on a breakaway in the second game and celebrated right in front of the Utah bench while hurling some well-chosen taunts at their coach—an ego boost of sorts. I knew they had made it their other primary goal to prevent me from scoring in the series at any cost.

I didn't even get to witness the most memorable part of the series because I was too far up the ice. Keven Brahmbhatt, a senior on the team and one of my roommates, apparently swung his stick like a baseball bat at a Utah player in the third period of the second game. The player was not touched, but you just never see stuff like that happen in hockey much anymore. Keven, who is Indian, had finally had enough of the Utah players yelling racial slurs at him all game and took a swing. He was kicked out of the game and suspended by the ACHA for the rest of the season, but nothing happened to the Utah team for the racist behavior that led to the incident. I felt bad that Keven, a senior, was ending his UW hockey career this way. I never understood why no action was taken against the Utah team for their part in the incident.

These games brought a poor first half of the season to a tumultuous end. Personally, my stats were right on pace with the previous season, but the team needed a spark. Christmas break gave us time to regroup, refocus, and come back ready to turn our season around.

We did. For our first games back, we flew to Tempe, Arizona, to play ASU—not only the best road trip of the year, but the best trip of my hockey career off the ice. I don't think there is a better place to go on the road for a weekend series than ASU. The weather stayed hot, and we quenched our thirst at the bars around the ASU campus.

ASU was arguably the best team in the conference besides Utah. They had a lot of skill, and they weren't jerks on the ice like the Utah players, so they didn't take a lot of stupid penalties or create any skirmishes. We got blown out the first night, losing 8–1, but we fought hard the following night and almost pulled out a win before falling 3–2. Despite getting swept, we sensed a change. As a group, we all ratcheted up the play and the intensity—including me. I prided myself on always playing hard, but I had only two months left in my college career, and I wanted to do everything I could to end it the best that I could.

We came back home to take on Oregon, knowing we had to win both games to force the shootout. Unfortunately, we lost the first game in embarrassing fashion, 9–3. This loss was the kick in the pants we needed. We couldn't just let Oregon push us around like that, so the next night we took it up a notch and won, 7–2. Even though we had lost the series three games to one, winning the last game gave us a welcome boost of pride and confidence. I scored four goals in the win, which made for a fun after-party.

The following weekend was senior weekend against Cal. It would be an emotional time for my fellow seniors and me, playing our last home games ever at Olympicview Arena in front of our fans. We took care of business on the ice, winning 8–3 and 7–3 to get the sweep. Going out at home with victories felt great, and having my family there watching and being able to participate in the senior night festivities on the ice made the event that much more special. My parents had supported me so much throughout my hockey career, so I got the chance to publicly honor and thank them for all they did.

When I came off of the ice after my last home game, I didn't get into the locker room for about twenty minutes. A bunch of young fans greeted me, asking me to sign autographs and take pictures with them. I felt like a rock star. Seeing the looks on the kids' faces when I handed them a signed puck was priceless. I loved it just as much as they did. The experience showed me how much of a positive impact I could have on people I didn't even know. Even a UW sorority girl asked for my phone number.

We finished out the regular season in Portland against Portland State. They played their home games at the Portland Winterhawks venue, Veterans Memorial Coliseum, which we loved, as most of our games aren't played in professional-caliber arenas with more than twelve thousand seats. We swept Portland State, which had us heading into the PAC-8 Conference Tournament flying high on a five-game winning streak.

Our conference tournament took place in Lake Tahoe, California, where we stayed in a resort right on the lake that housed our whole team. Off the ice, we partied pretty hard—a great way to spend my last weekend of UW hockey with the boys.

We finished out the regular season in fourth place in the conference, matching us up with UCLA in the first round of single-elimination play. I knew we wouldn't lose that game; no way I was ending my career against them.

We ended UCLA's season with a 5–2 win, a good game for me with a goal and three assists. I apologized to the UCLA coach, Marc Francis, after the game for knocking them out of the tournament. He and I had developed a great relationship off of the ice after the all-star tournament my sophomore year, so I could joke with him after our games.

And then—Utah. Of all the teams to end my college career with, I wish it had been anyone but them. We all knew we'd be done after this semifinal game. We lost, 9–2, but I made sure I played my heart out.

We were down 4–0 in the second period, but Utah was called for a penalty, giving us a power play. I had played well up to that point but hadn't had any good scoring chances yet, and I felt this could be an opportunity for me to strike. Because I quarterbacked the power play, I usually stayed at the top of the umbrella-shaped formation. Once we had the power play briefly set up in the offensive zone, Mooner slid the puck across the point that I one-timed and rifled into the top right corner of the net over the goalie's glove.

I knew scoring on Utah would infuriate the players and coaches because their goal in playing against us was to shut me out. I'll be the first to admit that I had a big chip on my shoulder when it came to playing against them. I celebrated with my teammates and then pointed at the Utah coach and yelled at their whole bench as a I went by to high-five Jacob Gilmore in net.

The entire Utah bench jumped up and screamed at the ref when I did this, and he assessed me a two-minute unsportsmanlike conduct penalty about thirty seconds later. I found it hilarious how upset they were that I scored and then celebrated in front of them. It made my day knowing I ruined their game plan.

As the third period wound down, I started to face reality. My college career was ending, and while it had been a great run, I couldn't contain my emotions. Tears streamed down my face as I finished the game.

After the handshake, I left the ice—always the last one off before Jacob Gilmore. My dad stood near the door, and when I saw his face, I really lost it. We gave each other a big hug. He had been with me every step throughout my whole career. The tears kept coming as I sat in the locker room. I was sad that my college hockey days—and maybe my hockey career—were over, but proud of how I had played. I had given UW everything I had, and I think everybody in the locker room knew that.

Before heading back to Seattle, all the teams still in Lake Tahoe attended the league banquet. Utah won the conference title over Oregon in a chippy, unbelievably brutal game, a classic game for anyone facing Utah.

I assumed the banquet would go as it did last year. I would give a speech on behalf of the team, thanking my coaches, teammates, and recapping the season. Then I would pick up my first team PAC-8 award and we'd party into the night one last time as a full team.

It was widely acknowledged by players and most coaches that I was the best player in the league. I again led the league in scoring, as I had all four years. But when they handed out the second team awards, my name was called. Everyone in the room was shocked. Other coaches couldn't figure out how this happened.

This was a deliberate slap in the face by the organizing team of the PAC-8 Conference and the banquet—none other than the University of Utah. They gave me that award to turn the screw on me. When their manager handed me the plaque, I didn't want to take it.

I still had to take a picture with him, though, so I stood there, holding the plaque, emotionless. I could see the manager had a smug look on his face, as if to say, "We got the last laugh." I kept my emotions in check on the way back to my seat with the plaque. One USC player who got a first team award came over to me later and apologized, actually feeling guilty he had received this honor instead of me; it was a very classy move.

That moment of purposeful disrespect just served to motivate me more in my hockey career and in life. There will always be people who will want to bring you down, who are envious of your talent or work ethic or who don't think you are worthy. It is up to you to show them they are wrong. That was my mindset, and I have my parents to thank for instilling this value in me. That same mindset carried me after leaving BSM and when my girlfriend left. I now had other people—the coaches of Utah—who clearly didn't want me to feel successful. I would eventually prove what a mistake it was giving me that second team award.

At UW, I saw the hockey program gradually decrease in talent and ability, but team awareness and growth of the program had steadily increased. I still couldn't walk around campus with UW hockey attire on and expect people to know who I was, but at least more people knew we had a team. I couldn't show up to a party and tell girls I played on the hockey team and expect that to help my case either, but at least some had now heard of the program.

As for myself, I improved each season at UW, both in mental toughness and maturity. Many players who play at the ACHA level decline as their careers progress. They lose their intensity or drive and don't make the most of their opportunity to play at the ACHA level. However, some do move forward, and I wanted to be one of those, someone who never accepted playing below my potential. I wanted to make my mark at UW, knowing that setting records was possible at both the team and individual level. The goal was to put the UW hockey team on the map. We did this by making regionals, and with our team's record throughout my career, my record-setting numbers, and great efforts by my teammates, we made the team more visible.

Every team that played UW knew who I was coming into the game. Pro hockey was not on my mind at all until my season ended, but I believed I had set myself up to earn an opportunity. I had no idea at what league or level or how I would pull off this feat, but I knew something would come up. I was determined to get as far as many of the NCAA Division I hockey players I had played with at the youth level—if not further.

I took my fair share of heat from my teammates during my four years at UW. I was the player who got most of the attention, though usually nothing more than a photo with a fan, an occasional autograph after a game, or an article mentioning me by name. As captain and president, I had a lot of control over the team, which probably upset some players. But I could count on my family to give me perspective and motivate me to strive to be my best. My dad often joked that it took at least four points from me per game to guarantee a victory at UW. For the most part, he was right. I had many conversations with my parents and my sister about the attitudes surrounding the UW team and my role on it, relying on their advice in dealing with teammates and making difficult decisions. My father typically put me in the right mindset and on track by reminding me to look at the big picture and consider what was truly important. My mother steered me toward maintaining a positive and upbeat attitude, citing helpful info from the many books she read about building a strong mental attitude. My sister offered an outlet for me to discuss social aspects of the team. I knew I could count on them to be ready to listen and help me in any way, as they always had throughout my hockey career.

During my senior year, my social life remained about the same—a single man still looking. I did go out to bars with friends a lot during the season. Every Thursday we'd show up at B-Mart, a beloved bar that no longer exists. Since I knew the bartender, I racked up a couple of thousand dollars' worth of free pitchers of beer during the year. All I had to do was tip him. I even went to a handful of frat parties with the help of a couple of teammates who could get me on the guest list. If I were to do college over, the only thing I would change is that I would have joined a frat. If I had done that, I would have had more friends, and my social life probably would have been livelier.

Being single did give me more freedom. And while I enjoyed hanging out with all of my friends, I still hoped to find someone special to connect with.

CHAPTER EIGHT

The Real World?

THE SEASON HAD ENDED, AND FOR ALL I KNEW MY HOCKEY CAREER MAY have been over as well. I wondered what I would do now. I had hoped to play on the PAC-8 All-Star Team again in Philadelphia, which would have been a nice way to officially end my college career. However, not enough players from the conference committed to attend, so that was a no-go. I concentrated on finishing my schooling, graduating, and then looking to either join the workforce or play hockey. I knew I would be able to get a job because of my background and internship experience, but where that would be I had no clue.

Lucky for me, Keenan Smith, a sophomore on the UW team and one of my good friends, invited me to go with him and his parents to Puerto Vallarta, Mexico, for a week over spring break. I had never been to Mexico and wanted desperately to go but didn't have the funds. I asked my parents if this excursion could be their birthday present to me, and they paid for my flight.

The trip couldn't have been better. The Smith family treated me like one of their own. I went parasailing and Jet Skiing, and ate delicious Mexican food. Keenan, a frat star in his own right, made for a good partner in crime as we hit the clubs each night. On past spring breaks, I had visited colleges or returned to Minnesota to see my family or just stayed in Seattle. This was my first real spring break vacation. Keenan's father, Pat, was part-owner of the WHL's Seattle Thunderbirds, so he was pretty well-connected in the hockey world. Having worked in real estate for many years, Pat had a deal with a client to use their condo for this trip—a great place right on the beach.

On the second to last day of the trip, I received a friend request on Facebook from a Finnish man named Tuomo Kamppinen. Since I had no clue who he was, I deleted the request, thinking he either was running a scam or had accidentally clicked the wrong thing. The next day, as I packed for the return flight home, I received another friend request from him. It seemed odd to get another request from a stranger in Finland. I figured he must have a reason, so I accepted his request.

Five minutes later, my life changed.

I received a message from Tuomo:

Hello! I'm manager of Virkiä Hockey team in Finland. We are playing Finland4 league and we are happy that we have been able bring couple guys from ACHA D2 play here in Europe. I'm wondering your situation, would you be interested and/or able to play in Finland? This season we had John Wright from SIUE, 2012–13 Jake Coyle from Florida Gulf Coast and 2011–12 David Wyman from Utah State. Also your old teammate from Wildcats Ville Mattila is played in our team.

Of course I was interested, but I knew nothing about the team. I had never heard of them, so I did a little research online. They didn't play in the top league in Finland; in fact, they were in the fourth league, which didn't sound great. I assumed they wouldn't be paying me much, so thought I would pass on the opportunity. But the more I corresponded with Tuomo, the more internal debates I had with myself. I thought about Brian Gibbons from Utah State, who'd led the ACHA in points and went on to play professionally in Germany in the fourth and third leagues. He'd be a good guy to speak with, so I sought him out. He shared with me how he ended up playing in Germany, about his positive experiences, and encouraged me to make the jump to Finland, though he admitted he did not know much about the league or the team I was talking with.

I didn't know much about Finland as a country. I learned that the months I would be in the country would be dark, with just four or five hours of sunlight per day. A doctor I visited described Finland as "the suicide capital of Europe," which I found a bit discouraging. But I had grown accustomed to the often cloudy, short winter days in Seattle. And Minnesota, where I grew up, had winter weather like Finland—cold and snowy, which made for great skating outside on ponds. But I had moved to Seattle, in part, to get away from the long, frigid winters.

Lapua, Finland, had a population around fifteen thousand, as opposed to Seattle, which had more than six hundred thousand inhabitants at the time. I liked living in the city. There was lots to do and always new people to meet. Going to a small town would be like going back to where I grew up in Minnesota, but even more secluded. And only a few hundred people showed up to games, which were played in an arena that could only hold almost a thousand fans. That counted as a definite negative, since every hockey player, once they get to the pros, wants to play in front of a massive crowd.

There were other concerns, too. The team practiced three to four times a week but usually played only one game per week. The regular-season schedule for the previous season listed only twenty-four games, all within a few hours or closer to Lapua. This shocked me, as I expected a fifty-game schedule and travel all over the country. Their season had the same number of games as UW. I had hoped to play a lot and travel all over Finland, but it seemed I'd be spending most of my time in and around that tiny town. What was I going to do with all of my free time?

Of course, I could explore the area and the country, but I didn't want to be doing that on my own. I would want some friends. I knew I would at least have my teammates, but would they speak English well enough to become friends and be traveling companions? Finland has arguably the best education system in the world, and Tuomo said everyone on the team and in the town understood English pretty well, but some people spoke it better than others. While I found that encouraging, Tuomo suggested I learn some basic Finnish to help my own cause if I came to the team.

I wanted to try to work a part-time job in town so that I could increase my cash flow and keep myself busy. The team said I couldn't get a part-time job in town. I would need approval for a work visa, a process that apparently took months, so I wouldn't be able to legally work in Finland until the season wrapped up. I might be able to help out with some of the youth hockey teams and possibly drive the Zamboni at the rink and be paid cash under the table, but Tuomo couldn't guarantee either of these opportunities. Since I couldn't work in the town, I thought about what I could do to benefit my long-term future. I planned on looking into companies with remote work opportunities.

I figured I had more skill and talent than a typical player in the fourth division in Finland based on the research I did on past import players in the league. I felt that if I had been coming from a Division I or Division III program, I would have had an offer from a higher-caliber team. Since I played club, though, lacking a well-established reputation—as a team and a league—I couldn't expect much. Just the opportunity to get over to Europe, however, elevated my excitement.

I had done a lot of research during my college years about pro leagues in Europe, such as possible salary levels and which countries I would ideally like to play in. I remained realistic about my possibilities, not looking at any of the top leagues. I thought Germany, Sweden, France, Finland, and Denmark all would have been great places to go, with the lower Germany leagues offering the best pay due to their economy.

I had skated with a handful of players in Minnesota who were playing professionally in Europe, so I spent a lot of time looking up their teams and following their careers. *Let's Play Hockey*, a Minnesota newspaper delivered to every rink and hockey player around the state, always has a list of Minnesota-grown hockey players in the pros. I loved looking at the list and seeing which players made it where. My name could be added to the newspaper soon, and that made me feel pretty proud of myself. This was basically the bible for every hockey family and hockey-related person who lived in the state of Minnesota.

I never missed an issue of this paper and even wrote articles in it for the Minnesota Whitecaps, a professional women's hockey team that was home to a number of USA Olympians.

My mom was the general manager of the Whitecaps while I attended BSM, so I often went to games and wrote recaps for *Let's Play Hockey*. I got to meet most of the players and skated with the likes of Jenny Potter, Winny Brodt, Brooke White, Chelsey Brodt, Gigi Marvin, Julie Chu, Caitlyn Cahow, Angela Ruggiero, and others. They really helped me gain a lot of respect for playing the game. Watching them prepare for games, and seeing their precision and focus, gave me a new perspective on what it meant to play top-level hockey. Their work ethic resonated with me, and I understood why most of them were Olympians.

Another lesson I took from following the Whitecaps came from the players' demeanor. Women's hockey is largely overlooked, and attendance at their home games was pretty low, especially in the early days of the team. They'd average around a hundred or so people most games, with maybe five hundred on a good night. I found the lack of support and interest dispiriting. These were professional athletes who worked hard at perfecting their game, yet they couldn't get the public to pay attention to them.

But I know this lack of recognition motivated all of the players. They had that chip on their shoulder because they had been overlooked for virtually their whole career. I could see that fighting attitude in the way these women played on the ice and in the way they talked on the bench and around the rink. They had to have tremendous desire and drive to be playing professionally. And it's unlikely they were paid unless they had a sponsorship. In fact, I know most of the players had to pay to play on the team.

These women might have gotten a little glimpse of the limelight in college and then playing in the Olympics, if they were lucky enough to make the team, but outside of that, they went unnoticed. *Keep that chip on your shoulder*, I told myself. *That attitude will take you a long way just like it did for these Whitecaps players.* I will forever have the highest regard and respect for all of the players on that team.

I got as much information about Virkiä that I possibly could. The team helped me get in touch with Jake Coyle, who used to play on the Virkiä team, as Tuomo had mentioned, and I learned a lot from him. He played at Utica College (Division III) and then at Lindenwood and

Florida Gulf Coast, both ACHA programs, before making the move to Virkiä. Jake helped me understand how to talk with Tuomo and told me what to expect when I got there if I signed with the team. Everything he shared about the team and the experience seemed to be positive. Jake tore it up in the one season he played with Virkiä, averaging over two points per game.

Tuomo never sent me the contact information for the other two former import players from North America, and he never mentioned them in conversation. I thought nothing of it at the time, but looking back, there may have been a reason for that.

Tuomo then sent me the team's basic contract. I made my own amendments, and then went back and forth with Tuomo via e-mail. I found the negotiation process fun, but at the same time, I just wanted to get it done.

It took me about a month to agree to a contract that I liked and the team's board members would agree to. Before I signed, I Skyped with the head coach, who seemed like a fine guy. I spoke with him for a couple minutes. All I really understood him saying during the conversation was, "We need sniper, that's what we need out of you." I considered myself a playmaker rather than a sniper, but if that's what they needed, I could do that.

Working long distance with all the members of the organization proved to be a positive experience, as they could communicate in English, and they treated me very well, which I appreciated.

The final contract showed I would earn €500 (about $560) a month, with all of my expenses—meals, housing, travel, and hockey equipment—taken care of by the team. I'd get a €100 extra per month working with youth teams, and maybe I could run the Zamboni or take a side job around town to make a few hundred euros more a month. In the end, if all worked out, I would make around €1,000 a month, maybe a little more.

Part of my negotiations had included getting all of my hockey gear paid for by the club. I wanted to make sure I would look respectable out there on the ice with fresh new gear. Perhaps they found my insistence stronger than most players, but I'm glad I put it in writing.

Jake had told me he had made €300 to €400 a month. I negotiated to get more than that. Even so, I would be officially making only around €4,000 for an entire season, hopefully around €8,000 with a side job. This was a pretty low number, considering what I could have been earning at a regular job out of college. Then again, I wouldn't be paying for housing, transportation, or meals, so I'd have few expenses. I knew this experience would be worth more than the money I'd be paid, so I didn't mind the trade-off. I had the opportunity of a lifetime to live my dream. Who knew where it could lead?

Playing pro hockey in Finland took me to the level I wanted to reach. Time would tell if I could reach the next rung in my career and move up the pro ranks. If I never got any further, at least I knew I did everything I could. I would always be able to say that I played professionally in Europe. Not many people can say they made it that far.

For some reason, I never reached out to any other teams in Europe during this process in the spring. I didn't consider looking to an agent for help, either. These options just never occurred to me. Knowing what I know now, I definitely could have—and should have. I can say with 100 percent certainty that I could have found other options—potentially better ones—in different countries and leagues.

When I had the final Virkiä contract in hand, I wanted to sign it like every other college athlete turning pro does today: in a room with a backdrop displaying their college. I contacted the *Daily*, the University of Washington school newspaper. I had worked for the paper as a freshman writing sports articles, so I knew they had access to a lot of the Division I athletic rooms for press conferences and other events. They had me contact the athletic department, and I eventually signed my contract in a UW Athletics news conference room. I didn't have all the pomp and circumstance, though. It was just me, my roommate Keven Brahmbhatt, and the athletic facility employee who let me into the room. I walked into the room wearing the one and only suit I owned, sat down, signed the contract with my favorite pen, and had Keven take a few pictures of me to memorialize the moment.

I had just signed away a year of my life to play in Finland.

Then came the public fame surrounding my moving on as a player from UW. When I say "fame," I mean one feature story in the *Daily*. Evan Franklin, a reporter with the paper, interviewed me for nearly three hours, after which he wrote a great article. I also met with *Daily* photographer Kyu Han at Olympicview Arena to do a little photo shoot to accompany the article. My photo was featured on the front page of the newspaper and the article took up the whole back page. I made sure to grab about forty copies of the paper that day for family and friends.

During the contract negotiations with Virkiä, I was still looking for jobs in case the Finland venture didn't work out. I had a couple interviews with the Washington Athletic Club, which has a hotel, pool, spa, restaurants, conference rooms, sport courts, and more. People could live there. It had everything the wealthy clientele could want. I was offered a position as a full-time business development coordinator. I didn't know whether I should take it because I would be going to Finland by September. I decided to take the job, which started the first week of July. I wanted the job not only for the experience but also as a possible reference if I returned to Seattle. Plus, until Virkiä booked my flight—which didn't happen until the middle of August—I had no guarantee I would be going to Finland. I wanted to make sure that if for some reason the Virkiä deal fell through, I would still be moving forward with my life.

Following my graduation from UW, I planned a road trip to visit a few major national parks with some good friends from high school: Jack Lee, Michael Conry, Tanner Speltz, Dan Morizio, Thomas Egger, Michael Kruse, Sam Ziegler, and Patrick Krieger. I talked to them every day while in college. We all pushed each other and continue to do so today to be successful in life. I wouldn't be where I am without their support, drive, and motivation.

Jack, Patrick, and Thomas were unable to attend this extravaganza, but the rest of the guys picked me up in Seattle the day I graduated. They had started the excursion in Minnesota about three weeks earlier, moving through Colorado, Utah, Nevada, Arizona, California, Oregon, and then up to Seattle. We went on to Vancouver in British Columbia, Banff in Alberta, Glacier National Park in Montana, Yellowstone National Park in Wyoming, and Mount Rushmore in South Dakota before returning to Minnesota.

Traveling with my good friends and exploring the national parks and other areas in the Northwest gave me a welcome respite before heading into the real world. And luckily nobody was seriously injured or gobbled up by wild animals. At Glacier National Park, as we hiked around a bank, we suddenly came face to face with a scrawny-looking mountain goat standing right in the middle of the narrow trail. It was a deer-in-the-headlights moment for us. We weren't sure of the correct protocol for dealing with mountain goats, but we figured if we didn't make any crazy noises and just moved slowly, we'd be all right.

In hushed voices, we debated what to do. If we tried to walk around the goat, we would walk right off a cliff on one side or have to maneuver up a steep slope on the other. We chose door number two and scrambled up the side of the mountain, where we all stood thoroughly spooked for about ten minutes, planning our next move and who would go first. One by one, we sheepishly slithered our way past the goat, who stood in its tracks in the middle of the path, watching us without much concern the whole time.

After a short stay in Minnesota, I flew back to Seattle to start my job at the Washington Athletic Club. The two primary people I worked with, Mike McGurn and Max Reich, welcomed me and made me feel at home. I could not have asked for two better guys with whom to start my business career. The work I did wasn't anything spectacular, mostly working on Excel spreadsheets and filling in data, but I knew I had landed a job with great people around me. I would find it tough to leave.

I enjoyed my time at the Washington Athletic Club and definitely would have continued to work there if I hadn't had the opportunity to play with Virkiä. When I gave my two weeks' notice, walking into Mike's office and explaining the situation, Mike and Max both congratulated me and wished me well.

As I prepared to leave, many people asked me if I felt nervous or apprehensive about the coming adventure. I really didn't. I had spent my whole life in hockey mentally preparing for this dream. I loaded up my hockey bag, stick bag, another hockey bag filled with clothes, and a little duffle bag of miscellaneous items—my whole life reduced to just a few bags.

My family members hugged me as they dropped me off at Sea-Tac Airport around 5:00 a.m. and shared in the excitement of my embarking on this journey, no matter how it turned out. Going in, I set a goal to find another team in a higher division to sign with for the next season. I wanted my career to end on my terms, but if that were not to be the case, I wanted to soak up as much as I possibly could abroad. I was not going to waste this opportunity one bit.

PART THREE
THE FINNISH

INTRODUCTIONS

I MET RYAN IN 2015 WHILE WE WERE BOTH PLAYING OUR FIRST SEASON abroad in Finland; Ryan was in Lapua (in central Finland) while I was two hundred kilometers southwest in Pori. The two of us had similar backgrounds, had both studied economics in college, and had a few mutual friends. As a result, we immediately bonded and enjoyed getting together to catch up, discuss hockey, and most importantly, commiserate with each other about the difficulties of being perhaps the only two English-speaking North Americans in a hundred-plus-mile radius. We often shared emails or stories along the lines of, "It literally took me thirty minutes to find chicken at the grocery store yesterday," or, "All my teammates were in a sour mood, so no one wanted to translate our video session—I had no idea what our game plan was."

Being paid to play hockey overseas is an opportunity I feel incredibly fortunate to have had. The guys I met, the cities I traveled to, and the cultural experiences that came as a result were truly once in a lifetime. With that said, it was a long nine months away from the comforts of the United States. Having Ryan—who understood the day-to-day challenges of being an import on a team full of Finns (and someone who also knew what Chipotle was)—in Finland made my Finnish experience that much more enjoyable and is one of the main reasons he and I remain close.

—Pat Mullane
Porin Assat (2015–2016)

Coming from Latvia, I had never met anyone from North America until Ryan stepped into our apartment in Lapua, Finland. I didn't know what to expect out of him. Right away I saw he had pretty good game on the ice, but off the ice, not so much. When he would go on dates with girls from town, Ryan would come back always alone, and I'd say, "Back so soon? Not looking good for you."

Ryan would respond, shaking his head, "Hey, I'm playing the long game."

"You won't get a text back tomorrow. No way," I'd say.

"We'll see. I think it went fine."

Then, when he didn't get a text back the next day, I'd start our dinner conversation with, "No text back? Long game, my ass."

We formed a close friendship in Finland, going through the ups and downs of our season, that has continued on to this day. Ryan is a true friend, and I am very proud of him for all that he has accomplished.

—Arturs Ozols
Lapuan Virkiä (2015–2016)

CHAPTER NINE

The Land

I DEPARTED FOR FINLAND AT 7:00 A.M. ON SEPTEMBER 2, 2015. I WOULD not arrive in Lapua until the next night at around 8:00 p.m. It took three flights and twenty-two hours just to get to Helsinki—from Seattle to New York; then from New York to Reykjavik, Iceland; then from Reykjavik to Helsinki—a total of fifteen hours of flying and seven hours of layovers, thanks to the team's paying for an ungodly "within budget" flight itinerary.

Upon arriving in Helsinki and securing my hockey bags, I was picked up from the airport by Toni Peltola, a friend of the team who lived in the Helsinki area and spent three hours talking with me at the station while I waited for the train to Lapua. He shared his knowledge of Lapua and asked me many questions about hockey in North America. When I finally boarded, I lugged my bags onto a train packed with people. The luggage area corresponding to my ticket had no room for my bags, so I had no choice but to block the whole walkway of a train car. Every time someone needed to get past me, I had to pick up my bags and squish them on top of me.

I spent four miserable hours on that train. I'd had maybe three hours of sleep over the course of a day and a half. I drifted in and out of sleep during the ride, hoping I would be conscious when I reached my stop. I set alarms on my phone to be safe. Luckily, I got off at the right spot, and I'm sure all the other passengers were glad to see me go.

I hopped off the train and onto the mud surrounding the little Lapua train station—there was no pavement. At first glance, the town appeared just like it did on the internet: a lot of industrial-looking buildings and drab colors.

A couple of the team's board members, along with the import player manager, Jussi, picked me up in a red convertible.

Jussi pumped my hand, and said with friendly good humor, "Hello, Ryan! Welcome to the jungle!"

These guys sure were excited to see me. The bustling town had one main street, and I think I saw the entirety of it in the five-minute drive from the station to my apartment. I was so exhausted I barely heard much of anything they said as they pointed out the various "scenic" highlights.

At the apartment, I threw my stuff into my room and met my roommate, a Latvian named Arturs Ozols. A lanky 6-foot-5, the Baltic defender had a quiet demeanor, similar to me. I didn't know much about Latvia or its hockey federation, but I knew the country sat geographically close to Russia. As a result, I assigned him the stereotype I had heard of a Russian hockey player: highly skilled, emotionless, and the drinking ability to bury me. I kept an open mind and figured I would find out soon enough. My living arrangements had been described as a spacious two-bedroom, two-story apartment. *Not bad*, I thought before going in. And then, during my initial walk-through of the apartment, grim reality set in.

The apartment sat above an old burger joint that was no longer in business and emitted a pervasive musty smell. The living room had a few random nails sticking out of the floor, a rickety pool table, and a couple of couches and chairs. The fridge was filled with snus tins (a powder tobacco product originating from a variant of dry snuff in early eighteenth-century Sweden) and some Karhu beer—a classic hockey fridge. I didn't have an actual mattress but a thick foam-type pad on a bed frame about two feet off the ground. My bedroom window had a large crack in it so the breeze could waft in, and the top floor seemed to be a storage area for moldy old clothes and retired kitchen appliances.

As I lay on my bed and stared at the ceiling, I thought, *What did I just sign myself up for?*

It was an eye-opening welcome to pro hockey life outside of the United States. Then I thought it was much like my entire hockey career, just another unconventional journey.

I struggled with jet lag for a week, never able to sleep for more than four hours at a time. The ten-hour time change was a lot tougher to deal with than I had anticipated. But after several days, I settled into a better sleep pattern.

I had practice with the team the day after I arrived. Although I was excited, I felt nervous because I had so many questions: What could I expect when meeting the players and coaches? How would the practices be run? What was the level of play? Everyone got to the practice at least an hour early because, as I later learned, we would be fined at least €2 if we didn't. We all kicked around a soccer ball and warmed up outside at the school field across the street from our home arena. My teammates, with the exception of my roommate, whom I really hadn't spoken with besides saying hello upon entering the apartment the previous day, were all speaking in Finnish. Neither Arturs nor I could understand anything, but we picked up on some swear words we heard a lot right off the bat: *vittu* and *saatana* and *perkele*. Only a few of my Finnish teammates could have a basic English conversation with me, and I had learned only rudimentary Finnish. Despite this, positive body language from my teammates helped make me feel more comfortable.

Practice itself wasn't too strenuous, as we had a preseason game to play the next day in Ruoviso, an hour and a half away. I had been looking forward to that first moment getting out there with my new teammates. We ended up losing, 5–3, and I had no points. I started the game and played a bit on the power play. Personally, I felt I made some good plays, but the line didn't click. I didn't execute on the chances created by my line, and my line mates also did not capitalize on the attempts I created. It was frustrating, to be sure, but this being a preseason game, I found the many opportunities my line had to be encouraging. I also had never played with any of these players, so we had little communication or chemistry, something we could work to establish in the preseason. I could build off the first preseason game.

My favorite part of playing the first game was how the team handled every aspect. No more club hockey style—flying by the seat of our pants in chaotic fashion. Our team traveled by coach—a large, comfy, high-end bus—to the opposing team's arena. We arrived two hours early to prepare, then went out onto the ice about forty minutes before game time for warm-ups. Finally, we took the ice about five minutes before the start of the game. My teammates were all very skilled, which was not always the case at UW and made me a lot more confident in giving up the puck and playing unselfishly, the style I had grown up with and preferred. I knew I wouldn't have to do it all on the ice by myself. This was just like how professional hockey worked in the United States, and I found it refreshing to be playing in this environment.

One change I noticed in pregame was that many of my teammates were downing coffee. A filled coffee pot sat in the middle of the locker room, and many drank it between periods. I had seen coaches drink coffee before and during games in the United States, but not many players. I learned that Finnish people drink the most coffee per capita in the world.

Over the next couple of days, I explored my neighborhood and the town. I could walk almost everywhere I needed to go, including the arena and Marian Talli restaurant, which sponsored me.

I still hadn't spoken much with my new roommate, Arturs, but we began our bonding at the restaurant with Jussi by our side. My contract stipulated I could have two free meals per day at Marian Talli.

I didn't know what Arturs's deal with the club was, but I found out quickly. We walked in, and Pasi Suokko, the manager of the restaurant, greeted us. Pasi shared a few words in Finnish with Jussi and then greeted me, "Hello. Welcome to Lapua, Ryan. I happy to have you. I will show you around. You have deal for two meal a day, lunch and dinner, yes?"

I replied, "Yes, that's right." Arturs, standing right next to me, wasn't acknowledged, and Pasi turned and started to lead us toward the buffet.

I turned to Arturs, and said, "Why does he know me but not you? Do you not have a meal deal?"

He said, "No, I have nothing like this, what you have."

Naturally, I felt bad about that and offered to pay for his meal, but he declined. I knew right then that he was a stand-up guy, and we would be friends.

After being showed through the buffet line, we scarfed down our food, and Jussi introduced us to his Finnish friends. We fielded questions about ourselves for half an hour. Then Jussi set us free to walk the five minutes back to our apartment.

I dreaded asking Arturs questions about his contract with Virkiä, because that is private business. But I also felt like I needed to. I couldn't keep going to this restaurant every day like I planned, going through the all-you-can-eat buffet line with him, if he couldn't get the same deal I had.

Back at our apartment I asked. "So, why don't you have the meal deal like I have with that restaurant?"

"I had no idea, man. I didn't even sign a contract to come here."

"Jeez, so how'd you end up here?"

"I have friend from Latvia hometown who played here, Rihards Grigors. He said it could be good place to play as a young guy. I am just twenty, so I took chance to come."

"Oh, all right, cool. But you didn't sign anything to come here. Do you get anything for being here or what is your deal?"

He launched into an explanation, somewhat embarrassed, I think, about how little he had received: "They pay my flight tickets and give me this apartment and promise me a job from sponsor. There is no salary, and I just take Tuomo's words."

"Wow, how'd you agree to that deal? They are giving you nothing compared to me."

We talked for a couple of hours about our deals and how we ended up here. We both decided he was getting screwed, and we were going to see if we could improve his deal.

The next day, Arturs and I met with Jussi at Marian Talli for lunch.

"How do you like the food here?" Jussi asked.

"Can't beat it so far," I said as I munched on some potato balls and veal. I followed that with, "But can Arturs get the same deal with this place as I have? He needs it or he won't be able to eat with me every day unless he wants to run out of money."

Jussi looked at me and then looked at Arturs, sitting beside me, and said, "I will ask to the board tomorrow. They have meeting."

I felt like I had the power to ask for Arturs because of the deal I had in place with the club. We both knew if he asked for it, they would probably say no. If I asked, they may say yes, as they hadn't really said no to anything I asked for during negotiations.

The next night after the board meeting, Jussi texted Arturs to let him know he could get the two free meals per day at Marian Talli, just like me. I didn't realize it at the time, but my career as a player agent had just begun with a successful negotiation.

We had two preseason games that week, but before gearing up for them, I learned how to drive a Zamboni, which proved not too difficult, riding along a couple of times with the driver as he cleaned the ice. I didn't think I would have much trouble, but starting out, I may have run into the boards a couple times. The toughest part was learning what each button meant, because they were all labeled in Finnish. The club set me up to drive the Zamboni each Monday for five hours and then every six weeks for the full week. It was a fun way to make some extra cash.

We played our preseason game against S-Kiekko, the affiliate team one league higher than Virkiä in Suomi-Sarja. Virkiä played in II-Divisioona. It would be a good test for our team and for me personally to see how I stacked up. Ultimately, I wanted to move up to that level of hockey, during either the current season or the next one.

During the summer and again after this game, Jussi and the board members told me that I likely would get to play with S-Kiekko. I played fine against them, but again had no points and didn't execute on my chances. We lost, 8–4, although we were tied up until the last five minutes. Discouraged, I knew that I could play better. I might have been pressing too much, as I came in expecting to be one of the top players on the team. I knew I could be, but I hadn't shown it yet. It would take some mental digging and hard work, on and off the ice, to play how I knew I could. I looked forward to getting back to my good form.

Jussi invited Arturs and me to play in his men's league on Thursday nights, where we got to have some fun and meet more of the board members. We piled on the goals in their game, as expected, and planned on continuing to play with Jussi as the old-timers' season went along. I had a great practice on Friday that carried me into the game that weekend.

On Saturday, we headed to a game near Pori, about three hours away. My main goals for the game were to play with energy and have fun—two things missing during my first two games. I needed to enjoy playing and let go of the anxiety. As I sat on the bus waiting for the others to get on, one of my Finnish teammates gave us all a big smile when he said in English, "It's a great day for hockey!" I really needed to hear that and repeated it to myself on the bus ride. I'd chosen this life, this adventure, so I needed to have fun and enjoy it.

I did just that in our game. I scored on my second shift off a shot in the slot to give us a 1–0 lead. I then scored on a breakaway in the third period and assisted on the following goal. We won, 7–3, and I registered my first goal and assist in Finland, much-needed milestones.

I had two more preseason games to help gear up for the regular season. I felt ready to go, back to playing my best. I just needed to stay mentally sharp and keep a positive mindset for the upcoming week of games.

On Tuesday, we again won, 7–3, and I had another solid game, notching a goal and two assists. After the second period, the coach switched up the line pairings and moved me off the first line and to the second line. I had a lot more chances to score in the third period, but being moved off the first line felt like a demotion. But since I was one of the stronger players on the team, moving me to the second line could be a good idea. It would give the team more depth if I could produce there and would allow me to potentially have the puck more often.

Our last preseason game, at home, proved to be a frustrating 2–0 loss as we outshot the opponent, 52–26. Unfortunately, we ran into a hot goalie. Overall, preseason gave me a good outlook for the regular season, as I finished tied for the team lead in points. I figured the regular season would only get better.

Following the game, we all went to the team sauna. I found it awkward drinking with my naked teammates while they spoke in Finnish the whole time. As the night went on and the liquor was flowing, a couple Finnish players mustered up the courage to try out their English skills with me. I gave them an A for effort, but they had room for improvement. They could say the same of me, of course, as I knew barely any Finnish. Then we all jumped in the freezing cold lake, a team tradition.

After the sauna event, most of the team headed over to a local club in Seinjaoki, a town about twenty minutes away from Lapua where most of my teammates lived. I met a bunch of my teammates' girlfriends and other random people, but communicating was tough because of the loud music and the language barrier. Girls did not seem to want to speak English to me, no doubt self-conscious about their speaking skills. So that made my quest to meet girls tougher than I would have hoped. At the same time, Arturs and I didn't see much potential in the club.

I hadn't seen any girls yet my age walking around Lapua these first few days, which was a bit discouraging. I'd seen plenty of girls in Helsinki waiting for my train, so I knew they existed, but I didn't have a clue where to find them near me.

As we left the club and took a taxi back to Lapua I asked Arturs, "Have you met any girls in Lapua yet? I haven't seen any our age."

"No man, it's awful. I have seen some ogres, though, if you are into that," he smirked.

Arturs and I had been in the ghost town of Lapua for almost a month. We saw only older people and little kids walking around during the day—if anyone at all. While it was free, the food left a lot to be desired, lacking seasoning and any real flavor. But it filled me up. For fun, teenagers formed large lines with their cars and drove slowly around town late at night blasting loud music, or they hung out in the church parking lot and smoked cigarettes. We wished that our apartment was in Seinajoki so that we could be around our teammates more. With no car to go back and forth between the two towns and not making enough money to take a cab, we just had to try and make the best of our situation.

Arturs and I spent the week leading up to our first regular-season game in excited anticipation. We would play against Jeppis on the road, but on an Olympic-sized ice sheet—my first in Finland, as our home rink and all of the rinks we had played on during the preseason were smaller, close to NHL-sized ice. The extra space of an Olympic rink gave me more room to operate, a definite plus for my skating style. I thought all rinks in Europe were Olympic size, but that was not the case.

In the first period, I got hauled down on a breakaway, so the ref awarded me a penalty shot. I came down in a straight line slowly and fired the puck off the crossbar, almost sniping the goalie above his glove.

That rattled me a bit because I had the goalie beat; I just missed my spot. We ended up losing, 9–5, in a poor defensive display, and I finished with just one assist. Overall, I thought we were outplayed by a better team. My line specifically had three potential goals that we left out there on the ice. At the very least, though, I got on the score sheet in my first official game. Now, I wanted to settle in and lead this team. However, my life never seems to follow the plan.

The next weekend we had our home opener. To my surprise, neither Arturs nor I would be in the lineup. As the coach put it, "We want to give the young guys a chance to play right now." Hmm. *Well*, I thought, *your management paid for Arturs and me to be here, so that may cause a stir.* I sensed a power struggle going on between the coaches and team management, and unfortunately, Arturs and I seemed to be in the middle of it. I accepted the coach's decision, as I didn't really have a choice anyway.

During the practice before the game, knowing we wouldn't be playing, I really let loose, playing hard and not caring what happened—with the consequence that I nearly injured two players by smashing them hard into the boards. It ended up being the most fun practice Arturs and I had so far on this team.

We won our home opener by a score of 7–3 as Arturs and I froze in the stands sitting with kids from the Virkiä youth teams. For some reason, our arena registered around 20 degrees Fahrenheit inside, with no heaters or warming room for fans. The good news was that I ate free food in the lounge outside of the arena in between periods with the team management and club members.

Both teams played pretty sloppily, but Virkiä got the job done. We found out after the game that the team management of Virkiä was having a meeting, so we held out hope for something positive to happen in our favor.

Since the beginning of the regular season—just two weeks ago—I had played center, right wing, and left wing, and been paired with different line mates every practice. Were the coaches playing some kind of mind game with me? I wondered. Their strategy certainly seemed odd. Not dressing me for the second game of the season—the home opener—just added to the drama. I just had to keep my end goal in mind: to play my best and try to move up and find another team to play on for next season. I reminded myself to focus only on what I could control.

The consolation of being in the stands was that Arturs and I could scout out the crowd and maybe find a couple of girls to chat with. We spotted just one girl our age—the girlfriend of one of our teammates. Brutal. We made sure to walk through the main entrance of the arena five minutes before the start of the game to see if we would be asked to show our tickets to get in the door. We walked in, no questions asked, so at least a few people around town knew who we were.

I began to learn a lot about the lower leagues of professional hockey. Team management could be lackluster, and as a result, many teams lacked funding and organization. Evidently, this was a theme all across Europe. Arturs, who had played in the highest league in Latvia a season earlier, faced various problems with his team due to poor management and money issues. I got a taste of what he faced when Virkiä didn't pay my September salary until the end of the first week of October, and then only after I sent a couple of reminders.

It seemed like this team also did not market itself well, despite having more than ten different logos on our uniforms. The team wasn't getting nearly enough out of those sponsors to make a sizable dent in team expenses it seemed. S-Kiekko barely kept afloat that season. They had a US import player, Kevin Ray, and it was rumored that I was making more money than he even though I played in a lower-caliber league. S-Kiekko had been in debt already. A team in my league called the Red Ducks folded two weeks before the regular season began due to lack of funds. I could understand teams in other countries, where hockey isn't the main sport, struggling with funding. In a country like Finland, where hockey is the main sport, such underfunding seemed a little puzzling.

I noticed Virkiä's lack of marketing right away. I didn't see any players really promoting our team to their friends, as confirmed by the poor turnout for the opener. Virkiä didn't have a YouTube account until the season I played. During the summer, I had searched "Virkiä hockey" on YouTube but found only videos from other teams' sites from years before. Virkiä had very little exposure, and most of it was not that positive for the team.

I suggested to management that I was willing help in this department. I voiced a lot of ideas for bringing in extra money, but all I could
really do was recommend, not implement. I kept pushing for improve-
ments. We did sell some T-shirts, scarves, mugs, and stickers at home
games. They even sold a shirt with my name and number on the back.

Near the end of September, the *Players' Tribune*, a media platform
founded by Derek Jeter, published an article I'd submitted about my
journey to play hockey in Finland.

Being featured as a writer on their site jacked me up. So many big-
name professionals had written for the publication in its first year of exis-
tence. My story was released on the same day as a couple of features on
superstar David Ortiz. I loved watching him play, and having him as my
online companion for the day put a smile on my face. I received a bunch
of tweets from followers and even gained a handful on Twitter, including
notables like ESPN's John Buccigross.

Let's Play Hockey tried to reprint the article, but the *Players' Tribune*
would not allow it. Still, that exposure helped me create a little platform,
provide an incentive to write this book, and encouraged me to try to
continue my hockey career—or at least that is what I hoped for at the
time. I wrote the article to really shed light on ACHA hockey, as there is
so little information on it online despite its growth in recent years. Now
players who might consider a career in the ACHA or take a route similar
to mine would have more information to draw from.

During this time, a couple of hockey agents contacted me about
becoming their client. I wasn't really focused on finding another team
yet, since my current season had just begun. However, the fact they knew
who I was got me researching more about the different European hockey
leagues. I ended up knowing quite a bit about the leagues in Europe and
where players—both European and American—played before getting
there. I spent hours and hours on eliteprospects.com, an online hockey
database that has all kinds of info on players, teams, and leagues. So
throughout my season with Virkiä, I scouted out teams to potentially
contact or have an agent contact for me if I were to sign with one.

Both Arturs and I were back in the lineup for our third game of the
regular season. We could see by their body language toward him that the

coaches did not like Arturs's style of play. Not only was he an excellent skater, but he was an offensive-minded defenseman with a bomb of a shot around 95 miles per hour. They didn't like his free-flowing style and offensive mindset because they wanted him to focus on defense first. I played really well with him. The coaches appeared to be okay with my North American style of play, but it seemed like they wanted me to be more of a physical presence than a goal scorer—different from what they said when they first signed me in May. But I wasn't going to move up the ranks if I was just a grinder and hitter. I needed to score and put up points.

Arturs and I agreed we wouldn't really alter our game style drastically, but I did make an effort to try to make a few more hits. The coaches didn't communicate with us at all in practices, instead speaking only to the Finnish players. We weren't really surprised at this, not expecting much from them given the language barrier. Despite the clear disconnect Arturs and I had with the coaches, we tried to make the best of the situation and took advantage of every opportunity during practice. We would challenge each other as to who could score more goals during practice or make certain plays, depending on the drill we were running.

We won our game that week, 4–3, but I again had no points and played third line, so I didn't get many minutes. I felt I played pretty well but had nothing to show for it. The coaches must have agreed, as they complimented my play throughout the game, tapping me on the helmet or clapping—a change from the usual. I came off the ice disappointed, though. I knew I needed to be producing if I wanted my career to continue.

On my first shift of the game, as I made a move around a defender skating into the offensive zone, he clocked me good. I took his hit right in the chin, knocking my helmet nearly off my head. Luckily, I wore a face shield, or I'd probably have left the game with a broken jaw or missing teeth. Somehow, no penalty was called on that hit. I couldn't believe it. I wore a full shield because it was the only request my dad made when I signed my deal to go to Lapua. I knew if I lost a tooth or injured my face, he wouldn't be very happy. Corn on the cob would be tough to eat, and I figured he wouldn't be wanting to pay for fake teeth if something did happen, so I obliged.

Later in the game, I had a rush with the puck all the way from the left side of my defensive zone and deked around two players. As I came toward the goalie from the left-wing circle, the ref got in my way, and I lost the puck on the mini breakaway. I was on my way to scoring my patented goal—cutting across the left side of the goal crease to slide it into the far-right corner of the net or five-hole. Thanks to the ref, I never even got a shot off.

That was my only good scoring chance of the game, occurring midway through the second period. I successfully killed a few penalties during the game, which was the first time the coach used me in that situation. I loved playing on the penalty kill and had since I was in high school, when I played on the scout team in varsity practices. I prided myself on shutting down the best players on specialty teams. Unfortunately for me, it didn't matter how much I liked to kill penalties or how good I was at it, because I didn't get to do it much again after that game.

The upcoming week was one I enjoyed, as I could look forward to a couple new activities. First, I got to run the Zamboni at the arena all week, so that kept me busy. The Virkiä hockey association then set me up to start helping Ismo Siren coach a youth team. Siren was a former Finnish player in the Liiga with Ilves and also finished his career playing for Virkiä. The arrangement with the association called for me to act as the assistant coach, running about half of the team's practices and helping Ismo in the others. The youth team of eleven-year-olds practiced only a couple times per week, and the association agreed to pay me €100 each month. Arturs wasn't set up to help coach these kids with me. I asked Ismo when I met him before the first practice if Arturs could help out and he agreed, though Arturs wouldn't be paid. After the first practice Ismo ran the kids through, I thought he would have been my team's best player. He was in his mid-thirties and clearly still very fast and skilled. He spoke English and seemed happy to have my helping hand, so I really looked forward to working with him and learning from him about coaching.

Then I prepped for my game on Saturday in Vaasa against KoMu HT, where we would be playing in Vaasan Sport's home arena of the SM-Liiga—a decent rink for a change rather than the frigid barns we had played in for the past few weeks.

I scored my first career regular-season goal in our team's 7–0 shutout in Vaasa. My goal came off of a rebound from a shot at the point that I put above the goalie's blocker midway through the first period. It felt good to get that one out of the way. I then added an assist in the second period to give myself a multipoint game, and I did it without playing on any specialty units. I was disappointed about not getting to be on the power play or penalty kill, but I had no control over where the coaches put me. Putting up points was all I could do to help my cause.

Following the game, I went to a Beatles festival in Lapua with Arturs, Jussi, Jussi's wife, and a few other board members. I ate reindeer for the first time that night, and was surprised to find I would definitely eat it again. The crowd at the Beatles festival was all much older than me. Jussi fed me Finnish long drinks, a mixed drink consisting of gin and usually grapefruit soda, all night, which ensured I had a good time. I did meet a couple of ladies my age there; however, they were not the striking blondes I remembered seeing at the Helsinki airport and train station, but instead were rather large, one with dyed bright orange hair and the other with dyed jet black hair.

The next morning, I boarded a train for the two-hour journey to Pori to meet up with Pat Mullane, another American player in Finland.

I knew Pat through Fabio Ghironi, my favorite economics professor from my senior year. Before coming to UW, Fabio had spent twelve years teaching at Boston College, where Pat Mullane had been his student. Fabio was passionate about his teaching, but perhaps equally if not more passionate about BC hockey. At BC, he held his office hours in the school's home arena, Conte Forum, while the team practiced. He'd sit and watch while meeting with and helping his students. To this day, he tries to schedule his economics conferences around the United States to coincide with BC hockey games.

Fabio invited me to his house several times over the course of my senior year to watch college hockey games on TV. We watched all of the

2015 Frozen Four together, which came down to Providence College beating Boston University in the national championship. BC and BU hate each other; if BU had won, Fabio would have lost his mind.

When Fabio learned that I was heading to Finland to play hockey, he connected me with Pat, who had played the past two seasons in the AHL and ECHL but then made the move to professional hockey in Europe. He had an impressive college career as well, as team captain his senior year and winning two national championships at BC—a pretty big deal.

Pat and I had exchanged plenty of e-mails over the summer and during my first weeks in Finland, so I looked forward to meeting him in person. He got me a family ticket to his game, so I had a great seat next to where Porin Assat entered the ice. This was my first time attending a Liiga game. The game was played at a fast pace, with very little hitting, and the fans reminded me of those at a soccer game, yelling chants the whole time. I found the level of play and the atmosphere incredibly fun and invigorating to watch. Pat collected an assist in his team's 5–3 win over TPS Turku. After a forty-five-minute autograph session, we went to a local downtown restaurant, then to a hole-in-the-wall bar to grab a couple of drinks.

I really enjoyed the time we spent together, talking about each other's careers and just sharing our thoughts on life. We seemed to have very similar outlooks, which made the conversation easy and enjoyable. He even offered to give me some of his extra sticks to take back, but unfortunately, he had a left-handed shot and not right-handed like mine. I stayed the night at his apartment and returned to Lapua on the 6:00 a.m. train.

The following week, I practiced with the third line. I did not participate in any power play units again. I don't know why I expected to have an easier time earning playing time with this team. Maybe I thought because I was the highest-paid player on the team and one of two import players on the roster, I would be given more leeway and opportunity. The road to ample playing time would be just as hard if not harder than in any other period of my hockey career. I recognized that I wasn't consistently producing every single game, which I attributed to a lack of playing time—but I also blamed myself. It is tough to get in a rhythm when you are bouncing around with different line mates and not playing many minutes. There is more pressure to deliver on the few shifts you do have on the ice. I also felt that if I had been playing top minutes and specialty units, I would be having multipoint games pretty consistently. I had a higher point-per-game average thus far than almost all of the other players without playing big minutes.

We won our game that week, 6–2. I had an assist in the first period and a breakaway goal in the last couple minutes of the third period. I played a total of twelve shifts all game and played on the fourth line. I couldn't understand why they would move me to the fourth line, but that's what they did. Having a two-point night for the few shifts I had made me feel good. The coaches' decisions motivated me, and I showed that through my play, making a positive out of the situation. I thought, *F*** you*, to the coaches as I skated through the line, high-fiving players after I scored my goal. I wouldn't let the way the coaches were playing me bring me down. The only thing they could do was to not put me in the lineup. If they went to that extreme, I think they knew the team board members would protest; after all, they are the ones who picked me to be on the team. Or at least I hoped so.

Because our team was in first place, the coaches had more leeway regarding who they were playing and how much time they were giving Arturs and me. And we were only two months into the season, so there was no sense of urgency to peak as a team. If we had been losing or been in the middle of the pack, I think the coach would have put me out on the ice more.

During this time, I had read a few really great novels: one by Andy Andrews, *The Noticer*, and two by Paulo Coelho, *The Alchemist* and *Manuscript Found in Accra*. These three books put my mind in a great state to help me overcome the obstacles on the ice. Incorporating a goal of reading every day, I read before I fell asleep or first thing when I woke up in the morning. I could definitely get used to this relaxed lifestyle of playing hockey for a living.

Midway through October, I received my second paycheck, a wad of cash handed to me in an envelope, two weeks late. Having to remind board members to pay my salary was less than ideal as a player. They paid me in cash to save tax money. To set up a bank account for me, the team needed to file paperwork for my visa, an expense they wanted to avoid. I stashed all my cash in my room, which didn't worry me as I trusted Arturs and knew Finland to be a very safe country. I left my bike, provided by the club to get around town, unlocked outside every night all season without worry.

A couple of days after I received that payment, we played a game against Muik, the second-place team in the standings, at Komarov Arena, named after NHLer Leo Komarov. The locker rooms for the rink are housed in a separate building next to the arena, so between periods we had to walk outside to get to and from the rink. I'd never played at a venue like that before, but I liked it because of the unique design. In the arena itself, the temperature felt like minus 20 degrees, probably the coldest rink I have ever played in. I can't say I really liked that, but as a result, the ice was really hard. We played a fast-paced game, losing 7–5. I had two assists on third line and my best regular-season game to date with Virkiä. For whatever reason, I had the puck a lot more than in previous games. I also played right wing in a game for the first time with Virkiä. As a right-handed shot, I prefer the left side because I find it easier to cut to the middle and shoot or drive wide to the net. This worked out well, though, so I hoped the lines would stay similar for at least the next game if I stuck on the same line.

Arturs, still without a job and given less and less playing time, became increasingly unhappy and angry with the organization. He spoke with board members and made a passionate plea for ways to make money. While a couple of members said they'd look into it, nothing changed much for him. We did eventually get a job doing some landscaping work in town, but that job lasted only one week. Arturs again asked for more work, and when he was told they had nothing for him, he retreated to our couch, knowing he could not spend any money. I felt really bad for him. Thankfully we had the meal deal and our squeaky old bikes for free transportation in town. We weren't spending much money all season except for our own groceries or when we maybe went out to one of the two bars or one club in town after a home game.

Nightlife in town was nonexistent, so we didn't frequent the bars or club unless we felt like getting out of the hermit life we lived. The one club in town, Oscar, had been closed since the end of August and wouldn't open until January. The two bars were small and filled with middle-aged men. The only time Arturs and I went to the bars was if board members invited us to tag along with them. All the young people like me, if they lived in Lapua, went out in Seinajoki. Taxis to and from ran around €70, and we couldn't really justify paying that given our lack of funds.

In this relaxed lifestyle, with nothing much to do, I soon became bored with just lounging around during the day. I reached out to the Lapua school district and we decided I could help teach fourth, fifth, and sixth graders English and about the United States. This turned out to be a great move for me: a chance to become involved in the community and give back what I could to the students.

I love being around kids; I always have, ever since my days working in my mom's daycare and preschool. I knew a lot about childhood development of all ages, and children from many different walks of life attended her preschool. Teaching was a vocation I thought I might enjoy in the future, so I looked at this opportunity as a trial run.

My first day at the Lapua school, Keskuskoulu, went really well. I gave two forty-five-minute presentations about US culture, answered whatever questions the students had, and even signed some autographs. The students all could speak at least a few words of English and wanted to know my favorite things—movies, colors, sports, places, and so on. Both classes blindsided me with one question, though: "Do you have a girlfriend?"

I answered, "Not right now, but if I did, I don't know that I would be in Lapua, Finland." The students all laughed.

I went back to another classroom to give the same talks two more times that week. I took pictures with students and signed more than one hundred autographs on kids' arms, books, scraps of paper, and hats. I even received a cute note from a fourth-grade student saying, "Ryan, you are really nice—from Diana and Jenni." It's the best feeling in the world knowing you made a positive impact on others.

Unlike on my previous teams, most of my Virkiä teammates either had girlfriends, were engaged, or were married. I think it had to do with the culture of Finland and the simple way of life. My most romantic night of the month I spent outside admiring the northern lights with Arturs—a great setting, but not the right company.

My team didn't have a game on the upcoming weekend, due to an international break for tournaments around Europe, as hockey players competed for their national teams. I didn't understand why low-level leagues took these breaks, but it is still this way today. Instead of playing that weekend, I spent time on my computer, researching and learning about sports agencies. I also attended an S-Kiekko hockey game with Jussi and Arturs. Watching the game confirmed my thoughts about the Suomi-Sarja division in Finland in comparison to the II-Divisioona that I played in. Slightly faster and with more prevalent coaching strategy, the game was one in which both Arturs and I could definitely play and make an impact.

At the game, I negotiated my first unofficial Finnish sponsor with Jussi: Tasangon cookies. We agreed that every point I earned during the rest of the season would equal one big bag of Tasangon cookies. This all started because Marian Talli provided little cookies to eat while drinking hot chocolate or coffee after a meal. They had a large jar by the door filled with these cookies, and I got into the habit of taking a few home with me after each meal. One lady who worked at the restaurant didn't like that, and whenever she saw me, she would take most of the cookies out in the jar. So, thanks to the sponsorship, I would now have Tasangon cookies at my disposal.

At practice, I started to notice that my coaches smelled of alcohol. I knew they drank a lot—just like most people did in this town, with nothing else to do—but I didn't expect them to show up to practice smelling of booze. Being coached by what Arturs and I figured were borderline alcoholics made it tough to take them seriously. There were a few people within the Virkiä hockey team's management who probably needed to go into rehab. Whenever I passed by one guy's favorite bar, I'd see him there: at night after playing in Jussi's men's league, on a Friday just after dinner, on a Saturday afternoon on my way to the arena, then again later that same night. He seemed to always be at that bar. It was sad, I thought, but I felt like I couldn't do anything about it. Or if I tried to, I probably wouldn't get any playing time at all.

Starting in the month of November, my €100 for coaching Lapua youth hockey players had been split in half between Arturs and me. The association felt that was only fair, and while I agreed with the notion, that was not how my contract read. I was too nice to say anything because Arturs needed the €50 to live. I knew that if we both had agents, Virkiä would not be able to get away with how they were operating—or, at the very least, we would have had someone with clout advocating for us.

For our upcoming game on the weekend, I would be playing on the third line. The Friday before the game, I practiced with the fourth line after practicing all week with the second line, which puzzled me. But maybe that was the point.

Despite the mind games, I went into the rink each game feeling grateful. I'd think, *I get to play a hockey game today in Finland. How cool is that?* I felt a certain bliss that always kept me going throughout the season, no matter the situation.

My game-day routine began with eating a peanut butter and jelly sandwich. Then I'd head over to the rink a couple of hours before the game. Next, I'd cross the street and go into a dark, empty basketball arena—where the Kobrat pro basketball team played—to stretch and warm up while listening to Zara Larsson and Dr Dre's *Compton* album. For whatever reason, those two artists put me in a good mindset that year.

I also would listen to a recording I made with motivational thoughts, such as, "Be so good they can't ignore you." It sounds corny, but listening to these thoughts before the game helped me visualize playing well and locked me in mentally. The rest of my teammates warmed up playing with a soccer ball outside in the cold. I didn't do this much because I thought it seemed crazy trying to warm up in freezing weather. I thought you were supposed to be warm after a warm-up, but not in Finland.

We ended up winning the game, 5–1. I had four shifts in the last two periods of the game. It was brutal, but if they wanted to pay me every month to get cold on the bench, then so be it.

Jussi came over the following day to talk with Arturs and me about our situations with Virkiä. Jussi seemed puzzled about why we weren't playing much and advised us to keep working hard in practice to show the coaches we deserved more opportunity. Arturs was at the point—financially and with his playing time—where he had to either demand changes, accept the fact that this was the way it would be for him in Lapua, or leave and go back to playing in Latvia. I got little playing time at the moment, and it seemed possible that Virkiä could buy out my contract if they wanted to send me home—a scary thought. I didn't want to go home; I wanted to play hockey.

The following day, I met with a guy named Janne, the chairman of the Virkiä board. He had heard that Arturs and I wanted to come to the next board meeting they held so we could voice our concerns. Instead, he met me at the rink while I was running the Zamboni.

I didn't waste any words. "I wanted to ask you, how do you think I am doing with this team?"

He responded, "I think you are doing fine. Board has no problems."

While I was relieved by hearing that, I said, "All right, while that's good to hear, I'm not playing much, and that is why I am here. I want to play hockey and try to build my career, and I feel like I am not really getting that chance. Is a trade to another team in the league possible?"

Janne looked at me, took a deep breath, and explained: "Ryan, I understand you, but no, we don't do trades. In the board, we don't get involved with the coaches and how they do lineup. I want for you to have a positive time in the club and make big impact in town as an American. You mean a lot for our fans. We are winning and having good season, and that is most important on ice. I can't help with playing time, but we in board want you here."

While I wasn't happy with his answer, I considered my options: try to find a new team to play on in a different country and opt out of my current contract, or stick it out and likely not get much playing time. I didn't know what to do, but I thought I would explore whether other teams would want me for an acceptable contract.

I started e-mailing teams in Belgium, the Netherlands, and Germany, just to see if I would get any replies. I also reached out to an agent, and I decided to confront Virkiä's head coach, which I did the next day in the coaches' office: "Hey, Coach, just wanted to ask what do I need to do to get more playing time and make more of an impact on the ice?"

He took a sip of his coffee and looked at his assistant coach, who spoke no English, then back at me and said, "You need to play old-time hockey, like Eddie Shore." That line is used in the movie *Slapshot*. Putting it lightly, Shore was an over-the-top, very physical player from Canada, so the line sounded ludicrous to me. I had to hold back my laughter when he said it.

"All right then, Coach. Thanks." And I walked out of the room. Unbelievable.

I had been teaching in the school for four weeks and was loving it—the best part of my experience in Finland. I wanted to emphasize to the students that I was more than just a hockey player. As a local celebrity in the town, I could use my platform to make a difference and impress on these kids the importance of a good education. Growing up, whenever I had a chance to be around pro or college athletes, I came away inspired and motivated by the experience, because I looked up to them and wanted to be like them one day.

Joey Martin, who played hockey at the University of Minnesota and then professionally in the ECHL, was one of those players. He had grown up just a few miles away from my house in Corcoran. He came to Hanover Elementary School with the National Championship Trophy in 2003 and later taught me a few hockey tips. I felt I could be like Joey Martin to these Finnish children. I wanted to give back and repay the sport of hockey that had given me so much in my life, and getting involved in the schools and the community was one way that I could do this.

I started filming at the arena and around the town and putting together a highlight tape of my college and pro hockey career as well as a video of my life in the town. I thought it would be an educational opportunity to put video out on the internet showing what it's like to play at a lower pro level of European hockey as an import player. I had fun with it, and it took me all season to put it together on YouTube.

We won our game that weekend against He-Ki, 5–4, coming back from a 3–0 deficit going into the third period. I scored our second goal as I came down the left side and cut inside the defenseman, firing a shot through the goalie's five-hole. I played fourth line, so in total I had ten

THE LAND

shifts in the game. It was infuriating, but I scored in spite of the little playing time and still maintained my point-per-game average.

Life became a bit more difficult as the winter season loomed. It snowed for the first time on November 20—about six inches—which meant I wouldn't be riding around town on my bike any longer and instead had to walk everywhere. The food started to become almost unbearable, as the lunch buffet cycled through the same food every week—never offering anything new or different. Each night, we had two choices for dinner so far at the restaurant: a slimy-looking chicken sandwich with potato balls or a hamburger and fries. Arturs and I ate the latter six out of the seven days. I also ate what became an unforgettable atrocious meal at lunch I referred to as the egg brick—a rectangle-shaped combination of eggs and sausage that looked and felt like plastic and tasted like eggshells. It was nearly inedible. It became the norm to walk into the restaurant, scan the buffet, look at Arturs shaking his head in disgust at the options, then spot the Tasangon cookie jar, and say to him, "Looks like a salad and cookie day for me."

During this week, Arturs and I ran a Virkiä youth team's practice. Only six of the team's fifteen players showed up for an hour and a half ice time. We didn't run them through a normal practice and instead let them play games like three-on-three and soccer on ice for an hour, which is strenuous with so few kids. Finally, we told them they could get off the ice, as we could see they were exhausted. I guess they were having fun, as they refused.

So we had them do "Herbies," a brutal drill named after the legendary US hockey coach Herb Brooks: They would have to skate from the goal line to the near blue line, then back to the goal line, then to the red line and back, then to the far blue line and back, and then all the way down to the other goal line and back. Brooks famously had the 1980 US Olympic team do Herbies following a tie with Norway in a friendly game during Olympic trainings. I gave the kids the option to either get off the ice or do Herbies. These kids did this drill for the last twenty-five minutes of practice until the Zamboni came on the ice. I was waiting for a kid to come and slash me for running them through this, but nobody complained. They impressed me, as I had never seen anyone voluntarily stay on the ice to do this drill.

I really enjoyed coaching these eleven-year-olds throughout the season and got to know a couple of them pretty well. One of them, Miko Tietavainen, wasn't the greatest hockey player, but he loved being on the ice. He spoke English the best out of all of the kids on the team, better than most of my Finnish teammates, so we had great conversations. He was a ball of energy, and I often would play keep away with the puck against him until he fell over on the ice. Olli Mäenpää, a much more reserved kid, always worked hard in practices and talked to me whenever he saw me in town. He spoke English pretty well and cared a lot about hockey, so I made sure to give him as many tips as I could.

In one practice after working with the kids, a peculiar thing happened. I was flying around and had scored a few goals in game simulation drills. Usually, when a player scores a goal, the coach would tap his stick, or I'd hear some hooting and hollering. He wasn't doing this for me today. If players messed up or didn't score, he usually wouldn't say anything. One time, I went down on a two-on-one drill and lost the puck trying to cut to the middle instead of just shooting it, as that likely would have been the smarter play. He yelled across the ice and mocked me, saying, "Hey, nice play Ryan, nice play."

The coach had never said anything like that at practice before to any player, so everyone on the ice was a little shocked. This confrontational behavior became the norm when we practiced. Clearly, he had a problem with me, but I felt at a loss as how to fix the problem. I didn't know anyone with any influence who would advocate on my behalf. I'm not sure what happened to make him start treating me this way. Looking back, however, I am sure the board told the coach about the conversation I had with Janne about my lack of playing time, which probably didn't go over too well and put me even further behind the eight-ball.

Our game that weekend didn't go well, as we lost, 5–1. I played on the fourth line again, so I didn't see much ice and registered no points. I did, however, finally fill out a visa application, sparing me from being deported from Finland after ninety days.

We had reached the first week of December. I would be running the Zamboni all week, so I'd at least have something going on to keep me busy. I wrote an article about my experience in Finland so far for the ACHA website, avoiding mentioning any of the negatives.

I had banner nights these days, where I watched a trilogy of movies called *Before Sunrise*, *Before Sunset*, and *Before Midnight*—romantic and thought-provoking films. I became slightly obsessed with them, watching each one multiple times and revisiting them in my head as the month went on. Living in the middle of nowhere in a foreign country and having no semblance of a love life caught up to me. Arturs struggled with the lack of a social life, too. By this point, he barely saw the sun most days. He routinely stayed up watching movies or playing games on his phone until nearly the early morning hours, waking up right before our lunch buffet closed up around 2:00 p.m. By then, the sun had already started its descent toward the horizon. I adjusted a couple of my nights to coincide with Arturs's habits. On those nights each week for nearly the rest of the season, we headed to our home arena to train. We both had a key to the rink, so we'd unlock the rink, turn on the lights, blast music from the speakers, and play around into the wee hours of the night. To this day, it is one of the best hockey memories I have. There is nothing like having a whole rink to yourself and being able to do whatever you want on it. And I had a great teammate to do that with in Arturs.

The following week, Arturs and I took a day trip to Helsinki to watch the Jokerit team play in a Kontinental Hockey League game, considered the second-highest league in the world. Jussi and Markus, a main sponsor of the club, joined us on the train down and supplied Arturs and me with plenty of long drinks and beer. Being in the capital and walking around in such an interesting and vibrant city invigorated me. I missed seeing streets filled with people and activity. The KHL game ended in dramatic fashion, with Jokerit beating Neftehemit, 6–5 in overtime. We didn't get back to Lapua until after 3:00 a.m. It was a long day, but well worth it.

We had a game a couple days later against He-Ki, where I played second line and was on the second power play unit, a welcome opportunity to get some decent ice time. We won the game by a lopsided margin,

15–5. I had a goal and two assists in the game, although on the score sheet I was given credit for only one assist, despite video evidence and the PA announcer saying my name three times over the loudspeaker. Even when I picked up points, I couldn't catch a break.

We had a team sauna event the following night as our Christmas party, where we all exchanged secret Santa gifts. I bought one of my teammates, who was in charge of team fines, a pink calculator and stickers. I received a Christmas-themed hat with bells attached to it. The night allowed me to interact with my teammates off the ice and get to know them a bit better, but because they all spoke Finnish most of the time, I made little progress. Arturs and I both continued to struggle to build good relationships with our Finnish teammates. We still couldn't have any sort of meaningful conversation with them. Admittedly, we have to take some responsibility for that, as neither of us had still learned much Finnish. I couldn't take a Finnish conversation much further that "*Moro mitäkuuluu?*" meaning, "Hey, how are you?" Looking back, this was an error on our part.

For the Christmas break in our schedule, I planned a trip to Berlin, Germany; Plzen, Czech Republic; Vienna and Salzburg, Austria; and Munich, Germany. I couldn't wait to get out of this tiny, provincial town. Before I left, though, the Virkiä board made me aware of a Christmas event at our home arena for the Virkiä youth teams. I thought it would be unique to have an English-speaking Santa, just like in the movies, handing out candy and asking children what they wanted for Christmas as they sat on my lap, so I volunteered to be Santa Claus. The Virkiä community loved that I did. Ironically, Rovaniemi in Lapland, Finland, is the official home of Santa Claus. I don't think my tall, skinny frame really fit the mold of a classic, short, stocky Santa Claus, but I did my best to improvise and give the kids a fun experience.

I exclaimed, "*Hyvää joulua!*"—meaning, "Merry Christmas"—all day. Then, in English, I asked, "What do you want for Christmas?" as each child came up to me, which was met with blank stares, as many didn't know how to respond in English. I tried to comprehend their Finnish responses, but thankfully the universal default Santa phrase, "Ho, ho, ho" bailed me out.

A day later my article about adjusting to hockey abroad came out on the ACHA website. I hoped that if there were players like me in the ACHA considering a shot at pro hockey, they would know they could reach out to me.

I also had two games over the weekend. We lost, 7–5, on Saturday, where I had one assist, and then we got smoked, 11–4, on Sunday. Though disappointing, these losses didn't bother me as much as usual, as I had my focus on my ten-day sojourn across Europe.

The trip brought a couple of highlights around the holidays. I spent Christmas with my old UW teammate Simon Machalek and his family in Plzen, about an hour outside of Prague. On Christmas Eve, we ate a traditional Czech Christmas meal of carp and potato salad and then opened presents. Simon's family gave me a bottle of Czech wine and a Jan Novak Czech hockey national team jersey. I couldn't believe they got me gifts, and I felt so thankful. Later, I shipped their family Virkiä team t-shirts, chocolates, and a thank-you letter as my gift.

On New Year's Eve, I went on a bar crawl with random people from my hostel in Munich for the night. I liquored myself up pretty well and managed to lose nearly all of the seventy people on the bar crawl halfway through, except for a couple of Americans and an Australian woman. As we wandered around the streets of Munich trying to find the rest of the bar crawl, we ventured into a train station. Immediately we were greeted by charging policemen, yelling at us to leave due to a terrorist threat in the station. All of the train lines were shut down, and I received text messages from friends back home asking me if I was all right because the threat made national news. Luckily, nothing bad happened, and I wound up finding a bed at my Australian friend's hostel.

With the trip coming to a close after a much-needed adventure, I felt a renewed energy as I headed back to Finland to start up the second half of my season.

Chapter Ten

Finnish Strong

Back in Lapua, life resumed as usual: days of practice, running hockey practices, driving the Zamboni, volunteering at the school, and playing a game on the weekend. Jussi informed me a team in Turkey had expressed interest in bringing me in for the remainder of their season. The pay would be double my current salary and the weather would be a little warmer than minus 20 degrees. Both of those changes sounded good, although the idea of Turkey as a country that loved hockey sounded crazy to me. Nevertheless, I waited to hear more.

We played KuRy on the road and won, 8–1. I had a goal and an assist on fourth line. In the second period of this game, I got caught on a long shift and could not get off the ice. The first line center and left wing had jumped on the ice. I found myself playing with Mikael Potila, who was our best player. I fed him a cross-ice pass, sending him in all alone on a breakaway and he roofed the puck for a goal. As we were celebrating on the ice, I said, "I should play with you more often," and Mikael replied with a smile, "Stay out long." Whenever I could, I did just that the rest of the season.

The next day, I went downhill skiing in Lapua with Arturs, who had never skied in his life. I consider myself an average skier, but Arturs had a lot of learning to do, and I had a few laughs watching him tumble down the hill on his first run. He looked like Bambi trying to learn how to walk when he attempted to get up. He didn't think the whole experience was all that fun—or funny—and called it quits once he made it back to his feet. I give him credit for at least trying something so difficult.

The following week, I booked a cheap weekend flight to Rome for the end of January, taking advantage of a weekend we had off due to another international break. I figured it best to get out of town and see some more of Europe rather than just sit in my apartment.

By mid-January, I still hadn't been paid my December salary. I assumed I would have been paid at the end of December if I had not been traveling, but no. Jussi felt my frustration, too, in a text exchange:

Ryan: Can you ask about December money and coaches money?
Jussi: I already asked maybe 5 times . . . Japi said that they dont have cash now . . .
Ryan: Oh ok. Ha so are they going to get cash anytime soon?
Jussi: Hope so . . .
Jussi: This sucks . . .
Ryan: I'm sure they'll figure it out at least I hope.
Jussi: Yes they will, but if you promise something . . . You have to keep it!
Ryan: Indeed.

Later that week, they handed me €235, less than half of what I should have been paid. Jussi explained that they would not pay me my full salary for December because I had not been in Lapua for the full month. I had been gone for less than a week and a half and missed no games or practices. Jussi also said that since I would be in Rome at the end of January for two days—missing nothing—they wouldn't pay me in full for January, either.

All I could do was shake my head.

My contract stated I'd be paid my full salary with no stipulations about being outside of Lapua, so I got into a bit of a battle with the board about the written contract. Simply put, they didn't want to pay me what had been agreed to in the contract. I reached out to a couple agents, asking whether I could pay them to help me with contract enforcement. Agents take a small percentage of a player's salary, typically a fee of around 5 percent in Europe. However, with my small salary and no agent having signed me to my deal in Finland, no one agreed to help me.

I then started asking other players I had met that season about how contracts were enforced. I learned that nothing could be done in any of the European leagues because the International Ice Hockey Federation doesn't take on little cases in lower leagues for small amounts of money. The country's ice hockey federation won't either, unless a team is bankrupt or breaking the law. Coming from the United States, where contracts (I liked to think) are generally honored and legally enforceable, I thought it would be like that everywhere. With European hockey, that is not the case. It is the same way still today, which can make having a good agent quite important. I expected an ugly dog fight at the conclusion of the season if I wanted to get all the money owed me.

For now, I cancelled my trip scheduled to Rome during another international break, throwing away more than €200. I had gotten approval for this trip from Jussi and other board members before I made the reservation, which is why I booked it, so this seemed a bit unfair. They did a complete reversal, claiming the week before my departure that if I went it would be a breach of my contract, even though there was nothing written in my contract about this. But I again learned that whatever is or isn't written in the contract, it doesn't always matter in Europe.

I wondered if Virkiä had shopped me to the team in Turkey because Virkiä wanted to get rid of me and my big salary. I didn't hear much more about this opportunity from Jussi, though, as the season progressed. I asked Jussi about it weeks later, and he didn't have any updates.

We played two big games on the weekend against Muik in a home series and were swept by scores of 8–5 and 4–2. I spent my time on the third and fourth lines. I had a goal in the first game but missed a penalty shot in the second game. I was 0-for-2 on penalty shots on the season, and I made the same move on both—came down slowly and shot high glove, but this time the goalie made the save.

After the games, my American iPhone died and wouldn't turn back on after charging. I had an indestructible CAT phone that the team had given me as a backup of sorts, but I only used it on the rare occasions a board member wanted to call me. I used my iPhone for all other communication, so I needed to get my phone fixed as soon as I was able. Jussi helped me find someone in Seinajoki to fix it, which took a couple of tries and nearly three weeks.

We played in Vaasa the following week, where we won, 7–6. I had one assist playing third line but sat out the entire third period at the coach's command. I didn't bother asking why, and I wondered where I would be in the lineup the following week—if at all. The second half of the season certainly had not gotten off to a great start for me, but statistically, I kept on my point-per-game pace despite the lack of playing time.

During the last week of January, our apartment seemed to have lost heat, and one night it suddenly went out. The overnight temperatures outside were below zero. We waited a couple of days to see if it would come back on, but it didn't. Arturs and I were freezing, and I would wake up at night shivering. I started to go to bed fully clothed, and that didn't do much, especially with my cracked bedroom window. I tried to get Jussi and the Virkiä board to get someone to fix the heating system a couple of times, but I never got any kind of response that week.

The following week, to combat the cold, I slept on a couch in the rink's office. I decided to go there because it was the warmest place I had been in town that I had access to at any time. Around 11:00 p.m., I unlocked the rink door, locked it behind me, and then made my way to the warm office to find the nice black couch calling my name. At 7:00 the next morning, I was awakened by the elderly woman who opened up the rink. Other than being a little stiff, I had finally gotten a good night's sleep. Arturs would have joined me if the office had more than one couch. He didn't want to sleep on the floor, so he stayed shivering in our apartment. A couple of days later, the apartment's heat magically came back on. We never knew why it stopped and then started again or whether someone fixed it, but we did wonder if we were being punished. Maybe the cold weather was making us feel a little paranoid.

Around this time, Jussi began acting very strangely, not being his usual helpful self. I sent him a reminder message about my payment for the month of January. His curt reply said he didn't have the money and that I should ask someone else about it. I found this puzzling, as his role on the team was to help the import players. I always got my money from him and even had him hang onto more than a grand in euros while I traveled over the holidays. It appeared he was done helping us; why, I didn't know.

Then we received this text from him a couple days later:

Jussi: Virkiä Hockey 2015–2016 is a f***ing joke! When these gutless f***ers will start play ice hockey? Nothing! Nothing happened this season so far! When I come to see the practice today, I see only lazy f***s. Doing nothing! No warm-up, nothing! F***ing stupid smiling! We will get smoked at the playoffs! Good attitude! Our import players should be our profile players! No matter what the others do. At the moment you can barely make the lineup! When the season started, plan A was that you play also at S-Kiekko. Well, they never called us . . .

Looking back, he really stopped helping us when we returned after Christmas break, so we should have seen this coming, especially considering I got paid for December twenty days late. Arturs and I continued to skate in men's league games every week—with Jussi—like we had all year long. It was an awkward situation. We'd get the occasional hello from him, but other than that, he wanted no part of us.

We had a game Saturday against APV, which we won, 4–1. I had a goal and an assist and Arturs had one assist. I played the whole game on fourth line, getting ten shifts total. That meant two cookie bags for me from Jussi, which I knew would agitate him. I found it kind of funny that he officially quit working with Virkiä the day after I sent him the message for the cookies he owed.

What I thought had developed into a good friendship did not turn out to be the case. It saddened me to realize that regardless of what kind of people Arturs and I were, and that we could have reflected well on him if we had been given more playing time, we didn't mean anything to him unless the board and the coaches thought highly of us. We thought he had our backs, but all along he sided with the team. I couldn't blame him for that because he worked for the team. This was an error in judgment on my part.

Since we considered Jussi a friend, Arturs and I probably talked too openly to him. He would always ask how we were doing and what we thought of the team, and we would be candid, not considering that he probably relayed everything we said to the whole organization. In retrospect, that is likely what happened all throughout the season, which probably explained some of the treatment we received from coaches and management. It was another huge lesson learned.

The next week we had two games against He-Ki. We won both games, by scores of 7–4 and 10–6. I had no points in the first game and two assists in the second one, though I was given credit for only one. I had missed out on a few points thus far, thanks to inaccurate scoring by officials.

But although my points were off, I sat fourth on my team in total points through the middle of February. If all my points had been counted, I would have been third. Pretty incredible for the rocky season I had with so little playing time.

Over the weekend, I started applying for jobs back in the United States and swimming at the community center pool with Arturs. I went into the community pool with Arturs wearing a typical American swimsuit that draped down to around my knees. Arturs wore his fashionable European speedo. As I neared the lap pool, a lifeguard yelled some Finnish gibberish at me, but I ignored him and hopped into the pool. We raced, doing laps for the next hour or so, and he swam much faster than me consistently for every stroke. His long, lanky frame gave me no chance to keep up. When I got out of the pool and decided it was time to hit the sauna, the lifeguard blew her whistle, and shouted, "*Et saa käyttää näitä.*"

I responded, "Sorry, I don't understand."

She paused to think of how to say what she meant to get across to me in English, saying, "This what you have on, do not wear. We don't allow this."

Then pointing to Arturs, she continued, "You must go to wear it."

I wanted to ask why, but I thought better of it, nodded, and left the pool. I wouldn't be going out and buying a Speedo to swim in this pool a couple more times while I was in town, so I decided if I went back to the pool, I would wear my American swimsuit again and take the wrath if it came my way.

At this point, I could feel my health going downhill. I had awful eating habits in Finland, eating two meals per day, once at around noon and then again at maybe 7:00 p.m. I wouldn't even take half of what Marian Talli offered at lunch by now because it was both unappetizing and not very healthy. Sometimes they served the same buffet food multiple days in a row.

Pasi, the owner of Marian Talli, treated Arturs and me nicely all throughout the season. We were both very grateful to him, especially the last couple of months of the season when things were not going very well. Eating at his restaurant was about all we could count on. After Christmas break, we asked for a new option other than burgers and fries for dinner, and Pasi put pizza on the menu. That became our new go-to evening meal, and we ate pizza almost every night for the rest of the season, with various healthy toppings like garlic, onions, tomatoes, chicken, sausage, and the like, which at least offered some variety. I had continued eating at Marian Talli only because my contract provided the meals, so I didn't have to dip into my salary to eat. But by early February, I felt I needed to start buying my own food—other than the occasional vegetables and fruits I'd been buying in an attempt to stay somewhat healthy—more often. However, I resented using my own money to buy food. Not only did that seem unfair, but I felt that if I paid for my food, my team was getting another turn of the screw into me. So I stayed on a mission to not let Virkiä beat me out of what they owed me. In retrospect, remaining healthy should have been more important than winning this battle.

I did meet with the mayor of Lapua, Arto Lepisto, for a nice public relations opportunity. I gave him a signed picture and spoke with him for about an hour about how much I enjoyed my off-ice activities in his town. He appreciated the kind words I had for the town of Lapua. I took a picture with him, which showed the people of Virkiä and those following the organization the positive impact I had on the town. He shared his appreciation with me for the contributions I made volunteering in the schools, coaching youth teams, being present for events, and giving my best to the town off the ice, which also made me feel a little better. Janne, the team chairman, probably felt good when he saw this picture.

We played APV in our second to last regular season game, but neither Arturs nor I were in the lineup. We sat in the stands and secretly cheered for APV to win. The choice seemed almost comical, especially since just a couple of weeks ago Arturs and I were instrumental in beating APV on the road. Not playing made me pretty angry, I'll admit. We won the game, 7–1, so the team didn't need us. Watching along with me and Arturs were most of the board members. They didn't acknowledge us or talk to us. Any time we passed by them on our way to snack on free sausages in between periods, they'd turn their backs or move away.

The next day, Arturs decided to ask for an airline ticket home to Latvia. He had been thinking about leaving for about a month, so I wasn't surprised. The powers that be granted his wish, and he left Lapua two days later—just like that. If I were him, I would have definitely made the same decision—probably even earlier than he did. We had built a great friendship hanging out every day together, so I was sad to see him go.

On Arturs's way out the door, I gave him a hug.

"All right, bro, I gotta come to Latvia and visit ya. Next season, though, I got you, don't worry. I'll find you a decent deal somewhere, so no more years like this."

"Yeah, man. Screw this team. But gonna miss you," he said, returning the hug.

I now had a two-bedroom apartment to myself—lots of room but no one to talk to. I'd go days without speaking more than a few words.

About the time Arturs left, the hallway in the apartment building began to reek terribly—like a dead and rotting animal carcass. I asked the board to look into it a few times for a couple of weeks, and they did, but nothing came of it. The couple who lived in the other unit in this building had moved out a couple months into our stay, so the smell affected only me. Any time I entered or left my apartment building, I had to hold my breath so I wouldn't inhale the awful stench. I later found out it was due to a broken pipe that left actual fecal matter in the basement of the building. After nearly four weeks, the management finally fixed it.

While the apartment complex literally smelled like crap, I thought about the top floor of my unit, filled with junk: boxes of clothes, old refrigerators, tools, tables, chairs, and the like—all moldy items you'd probably find in a hoarder's house. I wondered whether the apartment had been abandoned before we moved in. Given all the stored junk, the out-of-business burger joint, and now the broken pipe, that made some sense.

Thomas Egger, my friend from high school, came from London, where he was studying at King's College, over the weekend to visit me for our last regular season game in late February. He lucked out, having Arturs's bed to sleep in rather than the couch. I wished that I had more fun activities for him to do while in Finland, but I had no means of transportation at my disposal. The town did offer him the opportunity to cross-country ski while I practiced, but he got a good look at the simple, pretty boring life I lived in Lapua.

I did not dress for the game against IKK—the second game in a row I sat up in the stands. At least I had a friend to sit with. I was assuming my career would come to an end after this season and doubted I would play another game. IKK dominated us, 6–2.

Playoffs were up next, with our first round being the best of three against APV, who we edged in the regular season, two games to one.

Being the last week of February, my extracurricular activities came to an end: no more driving the Zamboni, coaching the kids, or volunteering in the school. I liked doing all three of these activities because it gave me a reason to get out of the apartment during the day, and I enjoyed interacting with the kids at the rink. I gave each player on the team I helped coach a signed picture of me with a little note saying thank you. If my season continued on for the next few weeks, assuming we made it past the first round of playoffs, I would have nothing to do during the day in Lapua.

The end of the month brought more than a little stress because Virkiä owed me more than €1,000, which included not only my February salary—which I'm sure they didn't want to pay considering I'd suited up for only two games the whole month—but also reimbursement for the hockey sticks I had bought. Virkiä had not paid for a single stick I used all season, although my contract stipulated the team would buy these for me. All season the board had promised they would give me that money, but I still hadn't received it.

For me, the first round of the playoffs had a lot riding on it because the outcome would determine when I could leave Lapua. I planned to travel around Europe after the season ended, but I couldn't book any arrangements until I knew how we did in the first round. Taking that trip meant I would have to store all of my stuff in Lapua with someone who lived there, because I didn't want to travel with all my gear, and I didn't trust Virkiä if I left my stuff in my apartment. I had a couple of people in mind whom I thought might help me. Ideally, I would return to Lapua after the trip to get my stuff and fly back to the United States. I also didn't tell anyone outside of my family about the trip because management had barred me from traveling the past couple months, and I knew there would be financial consequences if they somehow got word. I couldn't go on any social media platforms with my plans, in case anyone in town found out. All this coordination called for some serious strategizing.

Since we finished the regular season in fourth place in the division, we were awarded home-ice advantage for the first game, in which we beat fifth-seeded APV, 3–1, in a hard-fought game. I enjoyed watching the game in the stands, hanging out with the youth team I coached. The game had more intensity than those of the regular season, meaning more physical play. It reminded me a little bit of American hockey, watching players venture outside their comfort level. But it didn't come close to American-style hockey because any skirmish after the whistle or battle in the corner wasn't nearly as physical in comparison.

APV hosted the next game in arguably the nicest arena we played in all season. I'd hoped I would be playing in the game, but instead, I sat in my apartment and planned different scenarios for my travels. I imagined my current life to be very similar to being under house arrest: I lived at the mercy of my team to pay me before I could escape, travel, and finally be free to go home.

We ended up losing the second game against APV in overtime, 7–6, forcing a decisive game three the following day. I assumed once again, that I wouldn't be in the lineup. I hoped we would lose so I could get out of this misery and travel. However, the coach messaged me after the loss.

Hello Ryan you are in the roster tomorrow. Come ice hall 12.30.

While I know he wanted to get through this series without having to play me, in the end, by putting me in the lineup for the third game, he showed that he needed me for Virkiä to have the best chance of winning. I'm sure that frosted him.

My goal for the game was to capitalize on the opportunity to try to make the coach look like an idiot by not having me play the prior four games in which I'd been scratched.

Before I took the ice for warm-ups, our coach came over to me and said, "All right, Ryan, show me that I should have played you the two games before." I wanted to respond with a smart remark, but I just said, "Sounds good." Hearing his words confirmed to me that he knew I should have been out on the ice, but he had tried to win without me. His grudging respect, along with his challenge, provided a strong motivation to me, as I'm sure the coach knew it would. He didn't have to give me the chance to play at all, so I was thankful for the opportunity.

I made the coach look good and scored the game's opening goal in the first period playing on the fourth line: a greasy goal off of a rebound in front of the net after some cycling in the zone—textbook fourth-line shift. We won, 6–3, with an empty-netter. We clicked and played well as a team. That meant we would face the top seed, Jeppis, in the semifinals the following week. We had never beaten them in the regular season, so they would be a tough test.

After the game, I took a picture and chatted with one of my favorite kids, Olli Mäenpää, who I had been coaching all season. I was especially glad I had played in the game, because I knew Olli looked up to me and rooted for me to do well.

We opened with Jeppis on the road and enjoyed the fun atmosphere and stands packed with enthusiastic fans. The outcome of the game, we didn't enjoy so much. I played fourth line again, and we lost, 6–2. I barely played, having only five shifts in total—a chilly night on the bench for me. We were without our leading scorer and best player, Mikael Potila, due to an illness, which put us at a huge disadvantage. Mikael had played professionally outside of Finland previously in his career and also in Mestis, which is the second-highest league in Finland. He was skilled, creative, smart, great at protecting the puck, and the ultimate playmaker—the player who made all the difference offensively. He spoke English a bit, so I was able to converse with him at times, but I didn't get to play with him for much of the season outside of preseason. With game two up next, our team knew our backs were up against the wall. My back would just be leaning up against a wall, all right; I just didn't know if it would be in the stands of our arena during the game or on the bench.

The day before game two, I had job interviews with Google and Stanford Athletics. I would have been ecstatic to land a job at either, as both would put me on a great trajectory for my post-playing career. Funny enough, an article came out with Front Office Sports LLC about my job interviewing experience while overseas. I had reached out in February with the idea, suggesting it would be a good fit for their website, and they let me write what I wanted. I think my article in the *Players' Tribune* gave me the credibility for them to green light the article.

I expected a Jeppis blowout win in game two and wondered after my coach posted the lineup—with my name missing—whether I would ever play another game. I sat up in the stands with the Virkiä youth teams, watching a dominating performance from start to finish as we lost, 7–2.

A few hours after the game, I began implementing my exit strategy out of Finland. I needed to collect my February, March, and April salary from Virkiä, plus the stick money they hadn't given me all season long. I also needed to book all of my travels and make sure Virkiä would pay for my flight home, per my contract.

I collected my February salary the day before our one and only meaningless third-place game the following week to wrap up the season. I played on the third line because some of my teammates just didn't want to play in the game and sat out, forcing the coach to put me in the lineup unless he wanted to play a short bench.

I went in knowing that it was likely my last career game, but I didn't seem to feel any different. I simply focused on playing my best and trying to get a point or two so that I could feel good about ending the season. We lost, 6–5. I had an assist on our first goal of the game and then scored the fifth goal on my last shift of the game and last ever professional shift—the perfect way to end my career. I will never forget this special goal, where I played catch with Juuso Hakanen up the ice and one-timed a shot into the upper left-hand corner. I would miss playing with him, a very creative and solid defenseman with whom I had pretty good chemistry on the ice. I felt proud of myself after the game for sticking it out and finishing up the season.

I skipped the team sauna event following the game. I still needed to pack. My train left bright and early the next day to the Helsinki airport. I also didn't want to get questioned about the season and what I'd be doing next. By this point, I realized that speaking up and voicing my thoughts had backfired on me with Jussi, so I avoided being put in that situation. I didn't like laying low and keeping to myself, but I felt I needed to keep quiet about my trip and my thoughts on the season and beyond until I left Finland. I needed to make sure at the very least that the board would buy my plane ticket home, so I couldn't risk sharing any of my thoughts with teammates. I am sorry I felt I had to avoid my teammates and was uncomfortable expressing myself. It gutted me to leave the way I did.

The only people I trusted to discuss my plans with were Olli Mäenpää and his family, who kindly agreed to store my belongings while I traveled. I didn't share with them where I planned on going, but they knew when I would be back. They were great friends to me.

Finally, free of Lapua and Virkiä, it was time for an adventure. I embarked on quite the trip, three and a half weeks long, from Helsinki to Stockholm, Sweden; Copenhagen, Denmark; Amsterdam, Netherlands; London, England; Paris, France; Geneva, Switzerland; Nice, France; Milan, Italy; Barcelona and Madrid, Spain; and Lisbon, Portugal. I jammed as much as I possibly could into that trip, and I loved it.

Evidently the board had their suspicions about me and my whereabouts. When I landed in Stockholm, I already had a message from Tuomo:

Tuomo: *Huomenta!* Jussi and/or Arto brings moneys today.

We have problem, because flight supposed to be on Wednesday apartment rent is over this week and it supposed to be empty on Saturday.

Ryan: Ok. I'm not in apartment so that is fine. Can I have Jussi or Arto give the money to Timo Mäenpää.

Tuomo: So happy to hear that is not problem for you! I'll call to Jussi and ask him to contact Timo.
Ryan: Yep that works, sounds good.

Then Jussi sent me a message just moments later:

Jussi: Open the door
Ryan: Not home. Talk to Tuomo, he said he'd call you
Jussi: Where are you
Ryan: Went to Pori to visit my friend there
Jussi: When you come back
Ryan: Don't know
Jussi: We have to give the apartment away this Wednesday
Ryan: Yep Tuomo told me, all good
Jussi: You have your stuff there
Ryan: Nope, moved it out
Jussi: So we can go to apartment and clean it
Ryan: Yep
Jussi: Do you have your hockey gear
Ryan: Yep I'm all out

It was nice to see Tuomo say they had money for me. How much, I didn't know. What I did know was the club now was under the impression I had gone to visit Pat Mullane in Pori, had stored my belongings with the Mäenpää family, and hadn't decided when I would be coming back to town. Being proactive and knowing Virkiä would want me out of town as soon as they could paid off.

The trip had a few highlights. I wandered around the Red Light District for a few hours both nights in Amsterdam. I'll leave it at that.

Next, I visited Thomas Egger in London and went to a Chelsea versus West Ham Premier League game at Stamford Bridge. It was John Terry's 701th Premier League game played that ended in a 2–2 draw. I had always wanted to attend a Premier League game, and it was everything I hoped for in terms of atmosphere and caliber of play. The fans were crazy, chanting all kinds of vulgar cheers. I loved it. As I flew into Geneva, I took in the spectacular view from the Jet d'Eau. I made up my mind then if I moved to Europe it would be here or Salzburg based on what I had seen on my trips so far. Visiting here also made me think about how great it would be to share these travel experiences with someone special. *With a girlfriend, Geneva would be like heaven,* I thought. A few days later, I went to the Athletico Madrid versus Real Bestis soccer game in Madrid. This game had a different atmosphere compared to the Premier League game in London. Fans chanted all game long and for at least ten minutes afterward, but the cheering was not as ruthless or rude. Athletico Madrid won, 5–1.

That night El Classico, Real Madrid played Barcelona in Barcelona, which I watched at a bar near my hostel. Madrid won the game, resulting in screaming and raucous chanting in the streets. I had never seen anything like it. I capped off the trip in Lisbon before making the flight back to Helsinki. This trip served as a highlight of my life and my reward for all of the hard work in my hockey career.

Back in Finland, I took the train from Helsinki to Lapua, arriving around noon, which gave me time to take care of business. I planned to get the remaining money the team owed me, gather my belongings, and leave Lapua on the 7:00 p.m. train. I'll admit to being curious about how it would all go down. I arranged to meet Lauri, the president of Virkiä, at his electronics store to collect €1220 they owed me for my hockey sticks and my flight home. They technically owed my March and April salary too—€1,000—which they flatly refused to give me. I decided it wasn't worth the lawyer fees, time, and hassle, so I wrote it off as the price I paid for my "agent education."

As I walked into Lauri's electronics store, he greeted me less than warmly: "Ryan, where you been?"

"Hey, Lauri, I was just hanging out in Pori, nothing special."

"Apartment keys you bring?" he asked.

"Yes, sir, here you go." After I handed over my keys to the apartment, he grabbed an envelope off of his desk with the €1,220.

We talked briefly about the details of my flight home, and on my way out, he said, "Have a good life."

Not exactly the phrase I expected to hear, especially given the way I'd been treated, so I just had to laugh.

"Thanks. You too, Lauri."

I headed to the supermarket. No more free lunch in Lapua.

I bought a loaf of bread and peanut butter and jelly. I figured I could eat that for a couple days and save a bit of money. But I had no place to go eat the food, having given up the apartment keys. I decided to go to the rink and eat in the room I'd slept in that cold January night. I knew it would be warm and the door had a lock, so I thought I wouldn't be bothered. As I left the supermarket, I saw the Virkiä head coach walk in. I did an about-face, put up my sweatshirt hood, and went out the opposite exit.

As I got close to the rink, some kids I coached and a couple random fans spotted me. They started talking to me—asking me why I was still here and telling me about their season—until I finally escaped to the rink. Unfortunately, the code to the door of the warm room where I wanted to eat had been changed since I last made my way in. I figured Jussi switched it. So I went into the community center next door and hid in the bathroom, where I sat on top of the toilet and ate my sandwiches. I can't really explain why I felt so uncomfortable in the town at this point. I just did not want to be seen by anyone, explain anything, or say goodbye.

I decided to head over to Olli's house a little earlier than planned because I had made good time on my tasks. I gave his family gifts I bought in Portugal and packed up my bags, and then they drove me to the train station. I thanked them profusely and gave them all hugs, feeling lucky to have had their friendship and support. Without them I would have been in even more trouble in Lapua.

When the train arrived, a few strangers helped me carry my bags onto the train. However, the train ticket I booked happened to be for the following day. The ticket inspector came to me looking for my ticket minutes after I noticed.

I handed him my phone and he examined my ticket.

"This is wrong ticket, you know this?"

Playing dumb, I said, "Oh really? I am sorry. I didn't mean to book it how I did."

He then noticed my Virkiä hockey coat on, and asked me, "I am supposed to have you book new ticket. You are import player in Lapua?"

"Yes, I am."

He smiled and said, "Oh well. Everything is okay then. Have a good ride."

Thank you, Finland, for being a hockey country.

I had to transfer trains near the airport, which was a hassle, but I arrived at the airport around 11:00 p.m., fourteen hours before my scheduled flight back to America. I let go a big sigh of relief that I was finally on my way home.

I slept at the airport for only about three hours, lying across my two hockey bags, and woke up to my twenty-third birthday, April 8th. Because I was flying east to west, I had my birthday for about a day and a half, but oddly, didn't celebrate it with anyone I knew.

I thought about what I would miss leaving Finland. I would miss the practices, the late nights working on my game, hanging out with Arturs, my teammates, the locker room, the fans, and most of all, playing the games. I would miss the kids I coached and students I worked with in the classroom. I would miss traveling to and exploring so many new places and meeting all kinds of interesting people. I wouldn't miss the food, the language, the alcoholism, and the politics in the game.

Overall, I accomplished what I set out to do—with the exception of playing in the higher affiliate league Suomi Sarja. I played professional hockey and saw a lot of Europe. I made the most of my experience in Finland, and that made me proud. I did wish I had stayed in Helsinki for a few more days to really experience the city.

I couldn't believe I was on my way home. What I would be doing upon my return was yet to be determined, but I had some options in the business world. In total, the travel home took only fifteen hours—much better than the more than thirty hours it took me to get to Finland.

There aren't words for how happy I was to come home and see my family. It was the end of an era and the start of a new beginning.

I was ready.

Epilogue

I DID NOT TAKE A CONVENTIONAL PATH AT ANY POINT DURING MY hockey career, nor have I since. Following my season in Finland, I returned to live in Seattle, where I still am today. During my first pro off-season, I wondered if I would play again. I didn't seek out an agent to help me find a team for the next season, nor did I contact any teams on my own. Just thinking about playing the game of hockey mentally exhausted me. The European hockey market is built on statistics, and mine weren't eye-popping in Finland, so I knew I wouldn't have many options. Still, I guessed a couple of teams might be interested if I really wanted to pursue them. In late July, EC Lauterbach offered me a contract playing in the German Regionalliga, the fourth league in Germany. From what I had learned during my season in Finland, I knew it would be a much better living situation and that I would light up the league statistically, as it is a lower level than where I played in Finland.

I thought about the offer for about a week. I knew I could still play at a high level, given the opportunity. I also knew that the team would make sure to treat me well because they read my second article in the *Players' Tribune*, published in May, which detailed a bit about my season in Finland. In conversations I had with the EC Lauterbach coach and manager, they assured me I would enjoy a much different experience than I'd had in Finland. But despite the positive thoughts I had about the club, I declined the offer.

In the end, I decided it was time to hang up my skates and move on. I felt, given my history of concussions (how many concussions I suffered is unknown), it was in my best interest to take care of my body and prioritize my health. I wanted to be able to live a long and prosperous life, and I didn't want to risk another blow to the head. I wasn't making millions of dollars playing the game I loved, and I realistically would never get to that level. I'll admit, though, that I found the opportunity to live and play in Germany tough to pass up.

A couple of months later, I started my hockey agency—83, LLC—with my former roommate, Arturs Ozols, as my first client. Then I added his older brother, Kalvis. Then a couple of Finnish players signed on. This led me to branch out into North America. Over the past four years, I have built a successful and thriving business. In this short span of time, I went from just starting out to representing hockey players around the globe, and I have built a significant list of connections and a strong network all the way up to the NHL. Nobody thought I could do this, let alone be successful at it (except my immediate family). Many told me I couldn't do this, they didn't believe in me, and they laughed at the idea. But if there is one thing I have learned, it is that my unconventional journey is the natural path for me. In high school and even in college, I never would have thought I would be a player agent now. If I hadn't had all of the hockey experiences I had starting from age five through my time in Finland, I would not be running this business today.

Being able to help players from around the world navigate their paths from the bantam level all the way to the NHL is very rewarding to me. When a player is in a tough situation, I pride myself on being there, supporting them and providing them with guidance. I will always remember the helpless feeling I had in Finland when I wasn't being given much playing time, I had to fight to get my paycheck, and everything seemed to be going against me. I want other players to feel confident knowing someone cares about them, someone they can reach out to for help and support, especially in difficult and uncertain times.

I also want people to realize that no matter what path you take, whether it's the fast track or the long road, if you believe in yourself and don't give up, you can and will accomplish what you set out to do. My long and winding road of a hockey career is a testament to this, as is starting my hockey agency.

It certainly wasn't—and still isn't—easy, and I have a long way to go in my career. But I know I am on the right path.

I hope you enjoyed my story and that it can inspire you to achieve anything that you want to in life. I love helping people, which is what motivated me to write this book. Thank you for choosing to follow my journey.

Index